BUSES

YEARBOOK 2010

Edited by STEWART J. BROWN

Ian Allan
PUBLISHING

BUSES

YEARBOOK 2010

First published 2009

ISBN 978 0 7110 3399 3

© Ian Allan Publishing Ltd 2009

Published by Ian Allan Publishing

an imprint of Ian Allan Publishing Ltd, Hersham, Surrey, KT12 4RG.
Printed in England by Ian Allan Printing Ltd, Hersham, Surrey, KT12 4RG.

Code: 0908/D3

Visit the Ian Allan Publishing website at www.ianallanpublishing.com

Front cover: While Transport for London searches for the perfect double-decker its operators continue to invest in attractive, modern vehicles, such as this Alexander Dennis Enviro400 in the London General fleet. MATTHEW WHARMBY

Back cover (upper): The Optare Solo has been one of the success stories of the past decade. Here a Mercedes-engined M920 model pulls into Leeds bus station. STEWART J. BROWN

Back cover (lower): Markedly less successful was the Dennis Falcon V double-decker, of which just six were produced in the early 1980s. The East Lancs-bodied demonstrator is seen operating in Chesterfield in 1983. STEWART J. BROWN

Previous page: Although many independents have disappeared, West Coast Motor Services of Campbeltown continues to thrive. With the River Clyde as a backdrop, an Alexander Dennis Enviro200 stands in Dunoon in 2007. STEWART J. BROWN

Contents

Is Savile Row coming back into London fashion?

Alan Millar, editor of *Buses* magazine, considers London's ongoing quest for tailor-made buses.

LONDONERS HAVE LONG been convinced that the UK capital requires buses tailored specifically to its special requirements. Indeed, of many running themes to define the London bus scene over the past 40 years few have been as enduring — or as (so far) unattainable — as the quest to design its own double-deckers; a reluctance to accept off-the-peg vehicles when Savile Row is on its doorstep.

As I write these words in the first weeks of 2009, this movement has gained new vigour through Mayor Boris Johnson's competition to design a new London double-decker, combining new technology with a traditional rear platform and at least the appearance of a half-cab at the front. Culturally, this conviction has its roots in the earliest days of the undertaking that formed the bulk of what became the bus-operating wing of London Transport. One of the priorities of the London General Omnibus Co from 1908, when it merged with its two largest competitors, was to design and build its own buses. It was not alone then, for the fledgling motor-bus-operating industry was advancing faster than a manufacturing industry that struggled to meet its rising standards.

By 1912 LGOC's bus-manufacturing arm had become AEC — the Associated Equipment Company

London Transport traditionally sought standardisation and reliability in its bus fleet. The RT class provided it. Two examples are seen in Harrow in 1978, towards the end of their lives.
STEWART J. BROWN

RML2760 was the last production Routemaster, built in 1968. But, more than 40 years later, the type's appeal lingers, at least in the minds of some politicians. This is a 1980 view. STEWART J. BROWN

— whose close relationship with LGOC and London Transport from its formation in 1933 begat a succession of highly successful buses designed around the needs of London, though also eminently suitable for many other customers at home and abroad. This partnership's ultimate manifestation was the Routemaster, an integral-construction double-decker designed around a wide range of LT's strict operating and engineering parameters. It was conceived from 1947, tested in prototype form from 1954 and produced between 1959 and early 1968. While it was being produced it had extremely limited appeal outside London — just 50 buses for Northern General — and sold in significantly lower quantities than some contemporary products with broader customer bases. Yet it was an exceptionally durable product that, with refurbishment, lasted in front-line service for up to 46 years. Its survival, and LT's difficulty finding a suitable successor for its busiest routes, reinforced the argument that London still needed its own bespoke buses long after manufacturers tried to argue otherwise and even longer after all other operators professed themselves willing — perhaps even happy — to buy off-the-peg standard products.

London's conviction to the contrary was strengthened by its immediate post-Routemaster experience. As many *Yearbook* readers will testify, LT and its Swift single-deckers from AEC and its Fleetline double-deckers from Daimler and Leyland was a series of matches made in Hell. Depending on your point of view, either the buses were bad or LT failed to make them work. Some might say LT did

not want to make them work. The truth is probably a combination of some of the foregoing, but one reality is that LT was prompted to sell the new buses a lot earlier than first envisaged and to keep Routemasters running much longer than planned.

Manufacturers reacted to this by redoubling efforts to design better buses, with LT foremost in their thoughts. When the Leyland Titan and MCW Metrobus appeared in the late 1970s London was their key target customer, and, indeed, their biggest real customer. In the case of the Titan LT was almost its only customer, for its specification deterred most others from buying it new, though many leaped at the chance to buy second-hand examples when London started selling them in the early 1990s.

XRM is conceived — and killed

While getting to grips with off-the-peg double-deckers LT — or what you might choose to consider its fundamentalist wing — never gave up on the dream. Indeed, the last Routemaster had barely turned a wheel before a mock-up of an eight-wheel low-floor double-decker was being erected in the Chiswick Works. This hit the legislative brick wall of the Transport (London) Act 1969, which transferred LT's red buses and Underground to Greater London Council control and removed its powers to design or build its own vehicles — legislation passed while a

Labour government was in power. It regained those powers six years later and promptly revived its plans for an eight-wheel double-decker, which by now was called XRM. 'X' was for 'experimental'; no prizes for guessing what 'RM' signified or implied. LT's last custom-built bus was already assuming the role of a legend.

In the best traditions of 1908 the XRM was to be radically different from anything then available. The combination of eight small wheels and an hydraulic drive system would give it the lowest-possible floor with the greatest internal headroom. And by fitting an offside mid engine, it was possible to include an option with a rear door and staircase for the busiest routes, on which such a layout still held considerable appeal in London.

The side engine was an ironic choice, for AEC had tried valiantly to sell the idea to the British bus industry at large — and London in particular — in its Q-type single- and double-decker in 1932. By far the greatest number went to London Transport, principally single-deckers with an entrance behind the front axle, but LT also had some of the few double-deckers built, complete with a well-before-its-time layout of a front platform (open to the elements) ahead of the front axle and next to the driver. Had LT thought otherwise, the Q's layout

After the Routemaster London Transport tried a series of 'off-the-peg' buses, with unfortunate results. Here a broken-down Fleetline is passed by an MCW Metrobus, the latter type developed with London's needs very much in mind. STEWART J. BROWN

could have been developed into a radically different Routemaster, and London might have forgotten all about open rear platforms. But neither LT nor any other operator encouraged AEC to persist with this design.

Clever and unquestionably ground-breaking as all the essential features of the XRM may have been, they were unproven. Small wheels imply greater tyre wear, and the hydraulic drive was fuel-inefficient (at a time when oil prices began to soar) and at the cutting edge of technology. At the time only a Mercedes-Benz 'V' engine would fit into the tight space available under a centre staircase; this was neither common nor respected on British buses, and there were real political doubts that the GLC would ever countenance buying a German or any other imported engine for London's publicly owned buses.

Latterly watered down to a two-axle design with larger wheels, the XRM was becoming decreasingly financially attractive (or innovative) by 1981, when Sir Peter Masefield — the LT chairman appointed from a previous career as a senior executive in the civil-aviation industry — killed it off as a project too far. Significantly, given the bus industry's aspirations a quarter-century later, he did say then that manufacturers needed to make big advances in reducing the weight and fuel consumption of new buses. Nor did he close the door on the possibility that LT might commission its own new bus, suggesting a 'Super XRM' could follow in the 1990s when more advanced propulsion systems became available. But by then LT's plans for the XRM had started to look mildly insane from the perspective

XRM   Lightweight   Bus

By the late 1970s, against the background of growing dissatisfaction with Fleetlines, London Transport was working on the XRM project. Drawings showed different approaches, including the use of two or four axles, and alternative windscreen designs. The XRM would have had a side-mounted engine. LONDON TRANSPORT

X.R.M. Pictorial View

The side-engined AEC Q type — used as the basis of a small number of double-deckers in the 1930s — was one source of inspiration in London Transport's search for a new generation of double-deck bus.
ALAN MILLAR

of the rest of the British bus-operating and — manufacturing industry. LT had been talking of using XRMs to replace all of its Titans and Metrobuses from 1985 (many had not yet been built or even ordered) and of beginning to replace Routemasters only after that, but the markedly improved reliability of the Leylands and MCWs by comparison with the DMS *et al* made that aspiration appear almost wasteful.

V3 and Livingstone's GLC

Its new-found realism did not mean that LT had given up on the idea of a new generation of rear-platform buses. And, in a curious clash of objectives, it managed to have one built within a batch of new-generation double-deckers bought ostensibly to their manufacturers' standard specifications. In 1984 its Alternative Vehicle Experiment (AVE) programme brought into the fleet three Leyland Olympians, two Mk II Metrobuses, three Dennis Dominators and three Volvo Ailsas, and although by no means devoid of peculiar London features these were a lot less London-centric than the Titans or Mk I Metrobuses that had been bought since 1978.

The front-engined Ailsa was by then nearing the end of its production life after securing modestly successful sales, mainly from operators in Scotland. One of many missed opportunities in its earliest

years had been to offer it seriously to London, which, after all, had stuck with front-engined double-deckers almost to the last knockings of the breed in 1968. The Ailsa alone offered the possibility of a layout similar to that envisaged as an XRM option, with rear staircase and platform.

So while buses V1 and V2 were conventional by Ailsa standards, with front entrance, centre exit and forward staircase, V3 was a 65-seater with doors front and rear and forward *and* rear staircases. The theory was that it could operate like a Routemaster in the busiest part of the day, with back loading and a roving conductor, and at quiet times with a driver collecting the fares. And if the Ailsa itself was yesterday's technology, its Citybus successor, with mid-mounted horizontal engine and B10M coach components, could have a similar layout.

Maybe because it was the only one or because the layout did not lend itself to the safest driver-only operation — the rear door and staircase being a long way from the cab — the idea died a prototype's death. V3 was shunted off to the LT Siberia that is Potters Bar and had its rear door removed before an accident terminated its London career and almost its life.

Long before V3's demise LT was taking another of its periodical radical looks at the design of double-deckers. It had been returned from GLC to state control in 1984 following the political warfare between the irreconcilable Thatcher government in Westminster and Ken Livingstone's left-wing Labour administration in County Hall and was starting to look seriously at running all of its buses without

The unique Ailsa with two doors and two staircases, now in preservation. ALAN MILLAR

conductors. Three years earlier Dave Wetzel — Livingstone's ally and 'chair' of the GLC's transport committee — had come to power with a pledge not merely to retain the remaining conductors but to increase their numbers and build a new generation of Routemasters for them to work aboard. When I interviewed him in July 1981 this former LT conductor, driver and inspector was planning to establish a factory in London — in which the workers would share in the profits as well as the decision-making — to build a new generation of traditional double-deckers. 'We want a non-sophisticated front-engined bus, a bit like the old RT but with an automatic gearbox, power steering and heaters,' he told me. Correct me if I'm wrong, but at the time that sounded — and still does, nearly 30 years later — like the dear old Routemaster. He argued that a people-oriented public system would be better served by a return to such older standards. Politically, they may be poles apart, but I could just as easily imagine this last aspiration coming out of the mouth of Boris Johnson as that of 'call me Dave' Wetzel, who delighted in signing his letters 'Yours for Socialism'.

Ultimately Wetzel's dreams got nowhere, though the Greater London Enterprise Board — a quango set up by Livingstone's GLC to generate new employment in London — did acquire the wreckage of Ward Motors, the fledgling Yorkshire-based bus and coach chassis builder, after it collapsed in 1983.

Perhaps this was to be the building-block on which Dave's new Routemaster would have been manufactured, but political events moved too quickly for such plans to be developed further.

The Ogle interlude

State-owned London Regional Transport, as LT became in mid-1984, was talking of big advances in off-bus ticket sales and fare collection but recognised that even contemporary off-the-peg buses could be improved for London and to this end commissioned a new double-deck concept from Ogle Design, an automotive consultancy based in Letchworth with an impressive track record.

Ogle's PSV casebook included the Plaxton Panorama I, Panorama Elite and Paramount coaches as well as the similarly styled Duple Dominant. The jewel in its wider automotive crown was the Reliant Scimitar sports car, endorsed by the custom of Princess Anne, but it also deserved credit for two of the quirkiest cars of an earlier age, the Bond Bug and Reliant Robin three-wheelers, the latter immortalised as Del Boy's yellow van in the television series *Only Fools and Horses*.

Ogle did what any good objective consultancy would do and spent hours looking at how people used existing buses, taking these observations as the cue for changes to be made in its own new design. One of the things that this achieved was to rediscover the straight staircase, which had been a feature on Leeds buses before World War 2 and indeed had also been used in London. You can probably thank Ogle for the fact that this has become a compulsory feature of London buses since shortly after low-floor double-deckers arrived at the end of the 1990s. Many argue that a straight staircase is safer to descend than a spiral or angled one, though there is an art to be learned in climbing one as a bus accelerates away from a stop and you realise there is nothing to break a rearward fall; presumably the risks of the latter are considered less than those of tripping on your way down a spiral stairway.

Ogle's other major observation was that passengers approached modern buses and open-platform Routemasters in very different ways. It concluded that part of the Routemaster's crowd-shifting appeal lay in the fact that the platform opening curves into the back of the bus, enabling queuing passengers to board in three roughly parallel streams. On all newer buses the entrance is in one plane, limiting access to two streams, at best. Its solution was to design an asymmetric front for the next generation of London bus, with an additional door-leaf that would open up the nearside front corner to allow similar boarding arrangements as on a Routemaster but the other way around.

Dartmaster, Q-master and a stillborn Optare

Before there was much chance of Ogle's modifications manifesting themselves in a fleet of real buses the ownership and regulation of London's buses was being exposed to the possibility of more rapid change. Small batches of off-the-peg buses, bought for specific route contracts or for focused fleet renewal, became the new order of the day. Many of these were midibuses, like Dennis Darts, and the idea of a new London double-decker, be it styled by Ogle or by Prontaprint on the nearest suburban High Street, was off the agenda.

Yet the Routemaster would not die. Early in 1989, by which time LRT's bus operations, devolved to operating companies, were being prepared for privatisation, a programme was developed to refurbish the old girls for an anticipated 10-year life extension, the work entailing new engines and a major interior facelift. In parallel with this, perhaps to test the viability of the exercise, LRT also invited manufacturers to produce designs for a new fleet of half-cab open-platform double-deckers to replace Routemasters. Dennis offered a chassis with Cummins engine and ZF transmission, while Alexander and Northern Counties drew up designs based respectively on their RH and Palatine bodies on rear- and underfloor-engined chassis. As with XRM before it, this idea fell foul of the realisation that there would be little demand beyond London

for such a vehicle, meaning that — like the original Routemaster — it would be appreciably more expensive than rear-engined designs.

By 2000 life was changing again. LRT had become Transport for London, and the capital had an elected mayor in Ken Livingstone, who had returned to power older, probably wiser and certainly more pragmatic than when the GLC had been abolished in 1986. One of his lieutenants was the same Dave Wetzel who had been such a power in the land in the early 1980s, and once again there was talk of an expansion of Routemaster operation.

As a first step TfL was combing the land for old Routemasters it could reacquire and have refurbished with brand-new engines and gearboxes — the so-called 'Dartmaster' specification that transplanted the key elements of a Dennis Dart into around 40 of these 40-year-old double-deckers. Beyond that there was serious talk of a Son of Routemaster or Child of Routemaster — a new bus in the mould of the stillborn XRM that could combine conductors and open platforms with new technology.

Two bus designs attempted to meet London's aspirations. One was Q-master, the brainchild of Colin Curtis, who had worked on the original Routemaster and as a senior experimental engineer at LT was probably the XRM's most passionate ambassador. Long retired, he enthusiastically offered a side-engined bus with technology from an earlier age, such as an epicyclic gearbox and a big, normally aspirated engine. His styling drawings looked straight out of the 1950s, and the name went back 20 years earlier, honouring the AEC Q type.

The other possibility was offered by Optare, which had achieved great success and attention with some highly innovative single-deckers — especially the Solo midibus — that offered layouts and styling unavailable on the more conservative products of its competitors. It had yet to make a similar breakthrough with double-deckers but saw the possibility with its own side-engined bus conceived with London in mind. The side engine meant that it could have a flat floor throughout and allowed the same flexible door and staircase arrangements as on the XRM. Optare built its core products quite cheaply out of lightweight stainless steel, and on the one occasion that it revealed its thoughts on a driveline it talked of a Mercedes-Benz unit. The world had moved on since this seemed a weakness of the XRM, for Mercedes by now had a compact straight-six diesel that could do the job, and, indeed, was used widely by the largely privatised British bus-operating industry, not least in Optare products. On the one (different) occasion it showed

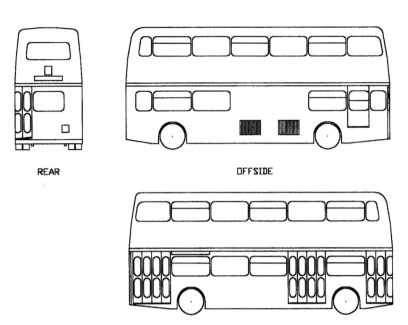

REAR

OFFSIDE

NEARSIDE

drawings of the double-decker to the specialist press Optare hinted at something more like a Neoplan coach than a typical double-deck bus, but there were rumours of engineering problems with the engine layout, and the idea never translated into three dimensions of bodied bus for sale.

Optare abandoned its plans partly because in the meantime TfL had prevailed upon Mayor Livingstone to think again, to recant his earlier, perhaps misjudged and certainly hasty

pronouncement that 'only a ghastly dehumanised moron would want to get rid of the Routemaster' and to replace the surviving examples with a wheelchair-accessible fleet of double-deckers and articulated single-deckers (or 'bendybuses') — a process completed by the end of 2005. Optare thus missed its chance, and TfL seemed content for its contractors to run off-the-peg rear-engined buses, albeit to a detailed specification dictated increasingly by TfL.

Boris and the bendybuses

Although most bendybuses were deployed in place of rear-engined double- or single-deckers — and most Routemasters replaced by double-deckers — the issue of bendybuses and Routemasters did not go away after the changeover, and a perception grew in the public's mind that the former had replaced all of the latter. This became one of the issues in the 2008 mayoral election, in which Boris Johnson defeated Ken Livingstone.

A key part of the new Conservative mayor's manifesto was to get rid of the bendybuses — to a Scandinavian airport, he suggested at one point — and to commission a new-generation Routemaster for the 21st century. His quest gained some strength and credibility when Capoco Design, a company responsible for a lot of the engineering design of such best-selling buses as the Optare Solo and Dennis Dart, published its ideas for such a vehicle in the Christmas 2007 edition of *Autocar*, the weekly car magazine. The RMXL looked quite like a Routemaster and adapted its lines and layout to fit a more modern bus-operating requirement, with hybrid or hydrogen drive, a low floor and separate (front) entrance for wheelchairs in addition to the obligatory open rear platform. As Capoco's Alan Ponsford commented at the time, this concept — then of a bus that looked unlikely to be built — generated far more media attention than any of the products its clients had built before in big four-figure numbers. The man who became mayor liked it, and it should perhaps be no surprise that a development of the RMXL was a joint winner of the competition that he and TfL held over the second half of 2008.

If TfL's professionals thought they were going to be able to neutralise Mayor Johnson's Routemaster ambitions in the way they had persuaded his predecessor, they would soon learn that they were mistaken. As well as announcing the competition within two months of being elected he confirmed that all Mercedes-Benz Citaro bendybuses would go by 2015. Undaunted by the additional cost of a substantial increase in the number of replacement buses and drivers, he sanctioned their removal from the first three routes during 2009, signalling that this was a process likely to be repeated with all future contract awards for routes using these vehicles. His intention is that at least one prototype 'New Routemaster' will be running by 2012, the year not only of the London Olympics but also, maybe more significantly, when the mayor faces his next election. Having an iconic new London bus to show will presumably prove that he has delivered on that promise from four years earlier.

The competition was divided into several different adult and children's sections, ranging from entrants' imagination of what a new double-decker might look like to fully fledged engineering designs. All had to fit within a brief specifying hybrid or similar drive, a low floor, wheelchair accessibility and a rear platform. The other joint winner among the fully fledged designs was a combined entry by the Foster architectural practice and Aston Martin, the sports-car manufacturer, which was one of few entries that succeeded in not looking like an AEC/Park Royal Routemaster. Indeed, many of them even came with Routemaster-shaped grilles and triangular badges capable of holding an AEC logo, while some tried to capture the shape of the back of the original model (sometimes with glass sliding doors), and one looked uncannily like a Northern Counties-bodied Barton double-decker of half a century earlier. All seemed to be driven by the thinking that a few years previously had led London Taxis International to create its TX1 black cab as an updated version of the 1950s FX4.

By inviting entries from designers beyond the normal community of bus manufacturers the competition provided a rare opportunity for some fresh thinking to be injected into British bus design, particularly by treating the interior from the perspective of users rather than manufacturers or operators. On the other hand this brought some features — a glass roof being but one — that seem unlikely to pass any practicality test. And by laying down the absolute requirement of a rear platform, it limited the scope for original ideas, a lot more nostalgia than clear-sky thinking being evident in the finished drawings.

Who might build it?

The design competition was only part of the process and in some respects has been a headline-grabbing sideshow. TfL also began seeking ideas from manufacturers about how they might develop and build between 700 and 800 New Routemasters over a three-year period. All three leading UK double-deck bus builders — Alexander Dennis, Wrightbus and Optare — were closely involved in this process, and it is possible that other potential builders might emerge in the UK or perhaps abroad. All could be expected to inject a lot more practicality into their designs, and although they were given access to the competition entries there appeared to be no compulsion for any of those concepts to be incorporated within the finished article.

One of the biggest concerns that remained was the perceived safety of an open-platform bus. One justification for withdrawing Routemasters from

all but the short 'heritage' routes in 2005 had been the increasing number of compensation claims being lodged — and accepted — over accidents in which passengers were injured jumping on or off Routemasters between authorised stops. If this were as big a problem as alleged, would it return with New Routemasters? And if it did, would operators or TfL meet the bill? Would manufacturers be held liable in court for producing buses that were less safe to use than those with doors? Or was the safety case overstated?

Another concern among manufacturers was whether, if TfL proceeds with its plan and commissions a new bus, the contract to build it will go to more than one of them. Between 700 and 800 buses is a prize worth winning, even if the buses are markedly different from all others built by the manufacturer and hold little if any appeal to operators beyond London. Priced realistically, the chosen builder could make a decent sum of money out of this order. But it becomes a lot less attractive if TfL hedges its bets and splits the order two or, worse, three ways. The precedent of buying all 400 bendybuses from Mercedes-Benz encourages manufacturers to believe that TfL would not be averse to awarding the work to a single contractor, even if that disappoints those who miss the prize.

This still leaves huge unanswered questions, primarily about the cost of such a project, how that cost will be met and whether TfL would countenance keeping these buses in London for 14 years rather than seven, as has become the norm for rear-engined double-deckers. Employing perhaps 1,600 conductors in addition to drivers will raise labour costs and pose challenges for London bus operators as to how they can minimise staff turnover in a job that for decades has had short-term appeal for those performing the task. TfL has suggested using Police Community Support Officers as conductors, although at the time of writing it has yet to become clear if this is a serious idea. It also believes that the additional cost of the bus need not be significant compared with that of a rear-engined hybrid, but manufacturers have yet to demonstrate just how low the price premium might be. On the other hand, if the new bus did prove that it could add to London's success in attracting ever-greater numbers of passengers onto public transport, that premium would be well spent.

What is clear is that this looks to be the best chance in more than 40 years of a bespoke London bus actually reaching prototype stage, maybe even of going into volume production. The bus-manufacturing equivalent of Savile Row may prove that it can be done.

Right: One of the joint winners in the competition to design a new bus for London came from Capoco Design. It managed to capture the essence of the Routemaster, even having a full-width cab.
TRANSPORT FOR LONDON

Below: The other joint winner came from Aston Martin and the Foster architectural practice and featured a centre door as well as the obligatory rear open platform, and stylish wheel-trims. Will whatever new bus hits the streets of London in 2012 be as stylish as the competition winners?
TRANSPORT FOR LONDON

Disappearing independents

Over the past 30 years many long-established independents have disappeared, some selling out to rivals, others simply closing down. **Mark Bailey** illustrates a selection of well-known names no longer with us.

Left: Based in the Somerset village of South Petherton, Hutchings & Cornelius served the area between Yeovil, Martock, Taunton, Ilminster and Crewkerne. Over the years a few double-deckers were operated, including a most unusual purchase in 1973 of a brand-new ECW-bodied Bristol VRTSL6G. A more typical vehicle, photographed in South Petherton in September 1978, was JYB 538N, a Plaxton Derwent-bodied Ford R1014. Hutchings & Cornelius closed down in 1979, four buses and most of the services passing to neighbouring operator Safeway Services.

Right: Lancashire United Transport served the mill towns and mining communities of south Lancashire, reaching Bolton, Wigan, Leigh, St Helens, Liverpool, Warrington, Salford and Manchester from depots at Atherton, Swinton and Hindley. With its roots in tramway operation in the early 1900s it grew to become the largest independent bus operator in the country in 1967. In postwar years it amassed a huge fleet of Guy Arab double-deckers, represented by late example 275 (ETJ 911F), a Northern Counties-bodied Arab V, at the Atherton head office in March 1978. LUT had become a subsidiary of Greater Manchester PTE in 1976 and would be fully absorbed in 1981.

Above: Berresford's was based in Cheddleton, Staffordshire, and was noted for its varied fleet of second-hand vehicles. It took over Byrne Bros of Leek in 1960 and W. Stonier & Sons of Tunstall in 1978, and retained both companies as separate subsidiaries. In later years it bought several Park Royal-bodied AEC Reliances from London Country, among them JPA 179K, seen in Blackpool in July 1980. Upon the death of Jim Berresford in 1987 the company was acquired by PMT.

Below: Based in Alsagers Bank, Staffordshire, Poole's Coachways operated a service from Audley to Newcastle-under-Lyme. Single-deckers of AEC and then Leyland manufacture were preferred, and a most unusual purchase was XFA 967S, a Leopard PSU3C/4R with Marshall Camair bodywork, seen leaving Newcastle-under-Lyme in September 1986. The Poole's business was sold to a local haulage company in 1987.

Above: The South Wales village of Tycroes was home to two significant independent operators, one of which was Rees & Williams. The main service ran from Llandeilo via Ammanford to Swansea, another reaching Llanelli. Leylands were favoured, an example, seen at the depot in June 1979, being LTC 107F, an East Lancs-bodied Panther PSUR1/1R new to Lancaster City Transport. The company was acquired by D Coaches in 1987 and in 1996 was sold on to FirstGroup, being duly absorbed by South Wales Transport.

Below: The principal route operated by Llynfi Motor Services ran from Maesteg to Port Talbot, being extended in the summer months to Aberavon beach. Leylands and AECs were preferred, and both single- and double-deckers were operated. Seen at Cwmavon in June 1979 is 149 (HRC 103C), an Alexander-bodied Leyland Tiger Cub PSUC1/11 which was new to Trent. Llynfi was acquired by the United Welsh group in 1988 and absorbed into the Brewer's fleet.

Right: Somerset operator Brutonian could trace its roots back to 1923, but acquisition in 1972 by Christopher Knubley marked a significant change in direction from coach to bus operation, and market-day services were run from Bruton to such destinations as Yeovil, Dorchester, Gillingham, Shaftesbury and Salisbury. One member of its interesting fleet was 497 ALH, a Willowbrook-bodied AEC Reliance new to London Transport, seen in Salisbury in July 1985. A further change of ownership followed in 1986, and Brutonian was eventually taken over by the Cawlett group in 1989.

Left: Trimdon Motor Services operated an extensive network of routes, reaching Durham, Houghton-le-Spring, Peterlee, Hartlepool, Stockton-on-Tees, Sedgefield and Bishop Auckland. From the early 1960s Ford became the chassis of choice, being superseded 10 years later by Leyland. Seen leaving Durham in June 1980 is OGR 653P, a Willowbrook-bodied Leopard PSU3C/4R. Deregulation saw an expansion into Middlesbrough and the creation in 1987 of the Tyne & Wear Omnibus Co, to compete in Newcastle; this was taken over by Go-Ahead Group in 1989 and immediately resold to Busways. In 1989 Teesside Motor Services was formed to continue the Stockton and Middlesbrough operations, and the following year this and Trimdon Motor Services were bought out by Caldaire Holdings.

Right: The South Notts Bus Co was based in the village of Gotham, midway between the termini of its main service from Nottingham to Loughborough. The 1950s saw the commencement of services, operated jointly with Nottingham City Transport, to Clifton, for a while the largest council housing estate in Europe, for which the company bought its first double-deckers. In the mid-1960s five Leyland-badged Albion Lowlander LR3s with Northern Counties bodies joined the fleet, among them 82 (82 SVO), seen at the depot in September 1977. South Notts would be sold in 1991 to Nottingham City Transport, which has retained its identity on a few vehicles.

Left: Hill's served the town of Tredegar and the upper Rhymney Valley for almost 70 years, but a significant expansion in 1976 saw it take over the large coach fleet of neighbour R. I. Davies. Typical of the service-bus fleet in later years was OWO 139M, a Leyland Leopard PSU4B/4R with Plaxton Derwent body, seen on the Tredegar town service in June 1979. Operations ceased in 1992.

Right: Connor & Graham worked into Hull from the coastal villages of Kilnsea, Easington and Withernsea. Seen in Easington in July 1980 is 69 (EKP 231C), one of a trio of Massey-bodied Leyland Atlantean PDR1/1s new to Maidstone Corporation. The stage services and the Atlanteans were acquired in 1993 by East Yorkshire, which completed the takeover the following year.

Left: South Yorkshire Road Transport, which succeeded South Yorkshire Motors in 1973, operated a network of services from Pontefract to Leeds, Doncaster, Barnsley and Selby. New double-deckers tended to be Leylands, and following the company name change there appeared a striking new variation of the traditional livery, sporting between decks what was probably the largest fleetname in the country. This is illustrated by 90 (HWR 690J), a Northern Counties-bodied Atlantean PDR1/3, in Pontefract in September 1979. South Yorkshire would be acquired by the Caldaire group in 1994.

Above: Based originally in Penycae, Wright's relocated the short distance to Wrexham c1980. A mixed fleet of new and second-hand vehicles, both single- and double-deck, was operated on local services and out to Chester, Llangollen and Oswestry. Seen pulling out of Wrexham bus station on the Penycae service in September 1985 is GCA 772X, a Plaxton Bustler-bodied Volvo B58. Wright's ceased operating in 1994.

Below: A1 Service was a members' co-operative serving the communities in Ayrshire between Ardrossan, Irvine and Kilmarnock. New and second-hand double-deckers were operated, and seen in Ardrossan in May 1990 is NCS 16P, an Alexander-bodied Leyland Fleetline FE30AGR (notwithstanding the Daimler badge) owned by Hill of Stevenston. A1 Service would be taken over by Stagecoach in 1995 and absorbed into Western Buses, and today some Stagecoach buses still wear a blue and cream livery in recognition of the strength locally of the 'A1' brand name.

Above: OK Motor Services was a sizeable independent serving the area around Bishop Auckland, in County Durham, and reaching Newcastle, Durham and Richmond. The 'OK' name was adopted in 1928 when the founder, Wade Emmerson, formed a partnership with Howe of Spennymoor, and this lasted until 1968, when Howe sold out. Leyland was the chassis of choice for new and second-hand acquisitions, and double-deck operation was commonplace. Pictured at the Evenwood terminus in June 1980 is FCD 286D, a Northern Counties-bodied Leyland PD3/4 which had been new to Southdown. OK acquired neighbour Lockey's in 1985 but was itself taken over in 1995 by Go-Ahead Group, which operated it as a separate subsidiary for several years.

Below: The original Blue Saloon of Guildford disappeared in 1938, but the name was later resurrected as the coaching arm of ABC Taxis. Local bus services were started in 1973, and seen in October 1979 is GRA 45C, a Neepsend-bodied AEC Reliance new to Chesterfield Corporation. Blue Saloon was to close in 1996, some of its vehicles passing to London & Country.

Right: G. W. Osborne & Sons was based in the Essex village of Tollesbury. The principal routes were those into Colchester, but Osborne's also served Maldon, Witham and Kelvedon. Coaches formed a large proportion of the fleet, but over the years an interesting selection of second-hand double-deckers was also operated. Seen in Colchester in October 1979 is 29 (GGM 431D), an ECW-bodied Bristol VRL — one of two VR prototypes with engine mounted longitudinally at the offside rear of the chassis. Osborne's was taken over by Hedingham & District in 1997.

Left: With its head office in Cranleigh, Surrey, the Tillingbourne Bus Co operated an extensive network of services in the Guildford, Reigate, Crawley, Horsham, Aldershot, Fleet and Farnborough areas. Apart from a few double-deckers bought latterly for an expansion into Wokingham and Reading all vehicles were single-deckers, many purchased new. Seen loading in Horsham in September 1998 is R203 YOR, a recently delivered Mercedes-Benz O405 with Optare Prisma bodywork. After over 75 years in business Tillingbourne ceased trading abruptly in March 2001.

Right: Cottrell's was based in the Forest of Dean and ran services linking Mitcheldean, Ruardean and Cinderford with the city of Gloucester, plus a market-day service to Ross-on-Wye.
The company occasionally bought new double-deckers, and pictured leaving its home village of Mitcheldean in June 1979 is CDF 204K, a Daimler Fleetline CRL6 with Northern Counties bodywork. Cottrell's gave up its stage services in 2004 and ceased trading altogether in 2007, ending more than 80 years of operation.

West Midlands interlopers

West Midlands PTE was the first English operator to place a large order for the front-engined Ailsa. **David Cole** and **Geoff Kelland** tell the story.

All photographs by David Cole

I N THE EARLY 1970s the UK's bus-manufacturing industry was facing challenging times. The 1960s wave of takeovers and mergers had left almost all production in the control of British Leyland — a politically inspired move which saddled the successful Leyland commercial-vehicle operation with troubled car producer British Motor Holdings. Resources were focused on the latter, and bus production was rationalised, limiting customer choice.

Further challenges to British Leyland came in the form of industrial unrest, both within the company itself and as a result of the three-day week imposed by the Government during the 1974 miners' strike. Production started to fall behind, and bus deliveries in the mid-1970s were often more than a year late. Production and availability of spares fell to unacceptably low levels, leaving operators with significant numbers of unserviceable vehicles.

Leyland's virtual monopoly of UK chassis manufacture was a matter for concern among some of the major bodybuilders, which foresaw the company's integral range — launched with the Leyland National — extending to double-deckers and reducing their market share, and consequently they sought new opportunities.

Working with Scania, MCW was first to market with the Metro-Scania single-decker, a competitor for the integral Leyland National. It followed this in 1973 with another Anglo-Swedish product — the Metropolitan — in its more traditional double-deck market. Not an unqualified success, this model nevertheless paved the way for MCW's long-lived in-house product, the Metrobus.

In Scotland Alexander worked with the recently established Ailsa Bus, a subsidiary of Volvo truck importer Ailsa Trucks, to develop an innovative vehicle intended to answer many of the Scottish Bus Group's concerns over Leyland's rear-engined products. This used the successful Volvo 6.7-litre turbocharged TD70 engine, which was compact enough to be mounted ahead of the front axle

alongside the entrance. Weight balance was optimised by mounting the Self Changing Gears semi-automatic gearbox remotely within the wheelbase.

The design was an early application of the now common perimeter chassis frame and was designed for an overall length of 32ft 4in (9.85m). Alexander's alloy-framed bodywork followed the builder's standard peaked-dome design but had a number of features specific to the front-engined chassis. These included a three-piece door which folded forward, creating more passenger circulation space aft of the engine, and a compact, forward-ascending staircase which terminated immediately behind the front upper-deck windows. This left space for three single seats on the nearside of the upper deck and had the added benefit of reducing the loaded weight ahead of the front axle.

The prototype Ailsa double-decker, christened B55 in Volvo's chassis nomenclature, was completed and tested in the summer of 1973, being formally launched at the Scottish Motor Show in November of that year. Ailsa had focused its sights on the Passenger Transport Executives as well as the Scottish Bus Group, obtaining a commitment from four of the PTEs to take the initial 10 production vehicles in 1974. Of these the first three were destined for West Midlands PTE.

The bus-operating industry had changed with the formation in 1969 of the first four PTEs and the National Bus Company. Each had inherited a diverse and often ageing fleet, much of which was unsuitable for the cost-saving drive towards one-person operation. For West Midlands PTE the preferred new double-decker was the Daimler Fleetline, as had been favoured by all but one of its constituent municipal fleets, but the large number of ageing half-cabs inherited, particularly from Birmingham and Wolverhampton, made dual-sourcing a necessity.

The initial second choice was the Bristol VRT, 200 of which were delivered in the period 1973-6. The PTE's challenges were compounded by the

acquisition in November 1973 of Midland Red's Birmingham and Black Country operations and the absorption in April 1974 of Coventry Corporation Transport, both of which brought further half-cab double-deckers.

The first three WMPTE Ailsas were ordered off the drawing-board without experience of a demonstrator and were from the initial production batch of 10. Numbered 4527-9 (TOE 527-9N), they were delivered in the autumn of 1974, entering service in December; prior to this 4528 was exhibited in the demonstration park at the 1974 Commercial Motor Show at Earl's Court. Bodywork was to Alexander's standard design for the Ailsa, with curved lower-deck windscreens, and seated 79. The three were initially allocated to Perry Barr garage and used on the Witton/Lozells services, a short one-man-operated rota which minimised the need for type training. No 4527 arrived first and was used for type training, including demonstration of the vandal-screen arrangements to the trade unions, which had been unhappy with the 'cage' arrangement on some of the Daimler Fleetlines.

The half-cab double-deckers acquired from Midland Red, to that company's iconic in-house D9 design, proved a particular challenge to the PTE when the availability of spare parts became seriously disrupted. The sourcing of additional new vehicles to replace them was therefore not surprising, although the choice of the Ailsa possibly was, given the limited experience which would have been gained from the

initial three vehicles when the order was placed. The order for 50 buses was the largest yet placed for the Ailsa, and early delivery was anticipated, although in the event there were some delays, and it was well into 1976 before the final vehicles arrived. The delays were, however, minor in comparison with those afflicting contemporary Fleetline orders.

West Midlands' production Ailsas incorporated a number of modifications in order to comply with the PTE's standards. These included flat windscreens on both decks, a revised interior layout and a relocation of the fuel-filler to the offside. The three original vehicles were never modified in this last respect, and care was required in placing the vehicles for the evening refuelling operation, as only certain pump lanes could be used.

Delivered between December 1975 and May 1976, the 50 production vehicles, 4738-87 (JOV 738-87P), were shared between the PTE's North (30) and South (20) divisions, entering service from respectively Oldbury (4738-67) and Sutton Coldfield (4768-87) — two of the garages acquired from Midland Red — and allowing many of the D9s to be taken out of service. At both garages the Ailsas were employed chiefly on trunk routes into central Birmingham. Oldbury was chosen by the North division so that the Ailsas could be allocated to the relatively easily

graded 87 route (the 'Track', from tramway parlance) along Dudley Road to Dudley whilst the capabilities of the type's small-capacity engine were assessed; they later appeared on a variety of routes, including the arduous 417 from West Bromwich through Blackheath and Halesowen to Hayley Green. The Sutton Coldfield routes were varied, scaling some reasonable hills in the more prosperous parts of the one-time Royal Borough, which was still smarting from its inclusion within the City of Birmingham in 1974.

Following delivery of the production batch the Ailsa model remained available for a further seven years, but no repeat orders ensued. The PTE did seek permission to order a further 35 in 1980, but the plan was vetoed by the County Council Finance Committee, which was anxious to safeguard local employment. Despite this in May 1981 WMPTE received a later Ailsa on loan for evaluation. Finished in full WMPTE Metrobus-style livery and given the fleet number 7054, TGG 386W was destined to be Greater Glasgow PTE A10, which fleet number it also carried. Built to GGPTE specification, it had a later style of Alexander bodywork, the R type, although the unusual interior layout, with no front seats on the offside of the upper deck, was perpetuated. Operating from Oldbury garage, often on the 87 service, it stayed until August before returning to Volvo Bus GB and then moving to Merseyside PTE for a short period of demonstration — still in West Midlands colours — before reaching its intended owner.

By the mid-1980s WMPTE was facing over-capacity and looking to rationalise the former Midland Red operations, wherein many staff had retained their previous terms and conditions (relatively unusual in those days, when it required the creation of a subsidiary company, but now enshrined in employment legislation). Sutton Coldfield garage closed in January 1984, and its Ailsa fleet was dispersed, 4768-72 joining the examples at Oldbury and 4773-87, together with the three prototypes, moving to Perry Barr garage but remaining on the same routes.

Early 1986 saw the closure of Oldbury garage, its Ailsa allocation moving *en masse* to Walsall only to migrate to Perry Barr later in the year. At Walsall they had replaced the last of the Bristol VRTs, but vehicle requirements were continually being reduced in anticipation of deregulation. Although all the Ailsas were finally allocated to Perry Barr not all were in service there at the same time, for the first three were withdrawn and stored in June 1984. They remained in PTE ownership when the PTE established its 'arm's length' operation, West Midlands Travel, but later passed to WMT for disposal.

At Perry Barr the Ailsas continued their association with Sutton Coldfield routes but could turn up on almost all the services operated.

Above: On loan as a Volvo demonstrator, this Greater Glasgow PTE Ailsa with Alexander R-type body was normally associated with the 87 route but is seen here in May 1981 on Birmingham's Hagley Road, operating on the more severely graded 127.

Below: During their brief sojourn at Walsall the Ailsas appeared on a wide variety of routes. By now fitted with a Vultron number display, one is seen in Wolverhampton in June 1986.

Exceptions (not always observed!) were the Outer Circle 11, on which there were concerns about the clearance beneath Handsworth New Road railway bridge (which now carries the Midland Metro), and the 90/91 to Hall Green, on which the Robin Hood Lane Bridge presented a similar obstacle.

Very few changes were made to the Ailsas during their time with WMPTE, the most noticeable being the installation of Vultron electronic service-number displays, which was undertaken at Walsall Works, where overhauls had begun in the early part of 1984. Following the transfer of the production batch of 50 buses to West Midlands Travel a local initiative by Perry Barr garage saw the commencement of a refreshment programme, including a repaint into the livery used on MCW Metrobuses. This featured more use of blue, of a brighter shade, and transformed their appearance. In this new guise 4739 was chosen to be Perry Barr's 'showbus' and made a number of rally appearances, continuing a tradition established earlier by Oldbury staff. Serious consideration had also been given to refurbishing an Ailsa (4770) which had been stored following an engine fire and repainting it into WMT's silver 'Timesaver' livery for use on the network of limited-stop routes introduced at deregulation. However, it was not to be, and, indeed, not all Ailsas would be repainted in Metrobus-style livery before the next phase of their lives began.

In the mid-1980s political changes in the capital prompted London Buses to seek significant cost reductions, achieved by an increase of one-person operation on suburban routes and the development of new tendered networks employing second-hand double-deckers. Besides reacquired DMS-type Daimler Fleetlines and a variety of MCW Metrobuses came 13 Ailsa B55s, with unusual Van Hool-McArdle bodywork, that had been new to South Yorkshire PTE. Of these last, 12 entered service at Potters Bar in the spring of 1987 and soon gained a reputation for reliability, whilst engineering staff appeared happy with what for London was a (very) non-standard type, so the opportunity later that same year to acquire West Midlands Travel's entire production batch of 50 Alexander-bodied examples, for just over £500,000, is likely to have been readily seized.

The last day of Ailsa operations by WMT was 7 August 1987, by which time the first examples were already running from Leaside District's Potters Bar garage; coincidently their final WMT depot and their first London Buses garage shared the same code (PB). They were repainted in the West Midlands at the premises of Brownhills Commercials, which

finished them in plain red with a black skirt and deep white waistband.

Following the ex-South Yorkshire examples and three bought new in 1984, the 50 West Midlands Ailsas were numbered in London as V16-65; however, in order to maximise correlation between fleet and registration numbers the later examples, JOV 766-87P, were given the lowest available class numbers, V16-37, leaving JOV 738-65P to become V38-65.

The 29 examples allocated to Potters Bar were to be found on the 84, 107, 234, 242, 263, 310 and W8 routes, the first, V52, entering service on 8 July 1987. All but one of the remainder had entered service by 15 December, the exception being V20 (the fire-damaged former 4770), which required rebuilding — by SBG Engineering in Kilmarnock — before appearing on 12 March 1988.

Elsewhere in London local networks were being tendered, and the remaining WMT Ailsas were allocated to the new Harrow Buses operation. A route network that had been retained by London Buses, this commenced operation from Harrow Weald garage on 14 November 1987. The 21 Harrow Buses Ailsas featured a brighter livery with a greater area of cream, although some soon gained additional red around the upper-deck window surrounds. A red 'HARROW BUSES' fleetname, surmounted by the silhouetted spire of Harrow church, was supposed to be applied at the front between decks, but the branding appeared inconsistent, some vehicles having London Buses roundels, and others both (or none!). The Ailsas were used on the key trunk routes of the Harrow Bus network including the 140 to Heathrow, as well as the 114, 183, 258 and 340.

The London interlude lasted around three years,

Right: In March 1987 No 4738 arrives in Birmingham on route 33, later to be one of the city's showcase routes. The bus is passing the now demolished Post and Mail building.

Left: Standing room only on 4744, carrying the later Metrobus-style livery, as it passes beneath Spaghetti Junction in April 1987.

Right: London Buses numbered the vehicles to match as closely as possible their registrations. Pictured resplendent in Leaside red, V57 was formerly WMPTE 4757.

the last Potters Bar example, V27, running on 27 September 1990, by which time all but one of the Harrow Buses vehicles had been out of service for several months; the survivor, V21 lasted into 1991, being retired on 11 January after service on route 340. Following withdrawal the Ailsas were moved to London Bus Sales at Fulwell, from where most found further users, just eight making a final one-way journey to Wombwell Diesels. More than 30 subsequent owners have been recorded, some vehicles changing hands several times. These operators were scattered throughout the UK, vehicles venturing as far afield as West Wittering, in Sussex, and the Highlands of Scotland, although many congregated in Yorkshire, and for a time Wombwell Diesels also used a few in its own hire fleet. Many vehicles achieved a full 20 years' service, at least one (4760, by now re-registered ANC 578A) still being used in the new millennium, by EMS Bus & Coach, of Greasby, on the Wirral. Several Ailsas returned to the West Midlands, and three ultimately found their way back into WMT ownership, albeit remaining unused. However, the largest and arguably best-known fleet of ex-London Buses, ex-WMPTE Ailsas was that built up by Black Prince of Morley, Leeds, which in addition to three acquired solely for spares ran nine examples for various periods alongside other Ailsas from London and Scotland.

Back in the Ailsas' original stamping-ground West Midlands Travel had become Travel West Midlands and was once again operating Volvo double-deckers in the form of Plaxton- and Alexander-bodied B7TLs, the first of which had arrived in 1999, nearly

a quarter of a century after the last new Volvo double-deckers. However, in 2002 the Ailsa B55 had one further role to play. West Bromwich Albion and Birmingham City football clubs had both won promotion to the Premier Division, and two open-toppers were required for the clubs' parades. Travel West Midlands had a suitable Metrobus, and the only other open-topper available within the National Express Group was Ailsa 300 from the Travel Dundee fleet. This Alexander-bodied bus had been new to Tayside Regional Transport in 1979, being retained for use on the Dundee city tour and named *Broughty Castle*. For its short stay in the West Midlands it gained appropriate fleetnames and fleet number 3272 to match its registration (WTS 272T). Sold out of the National Express Group shortly afterwards, it subsequently operated a sightseeing tour of Oxford before returning to Dundee for preservation.

In comparison with the much more numerous Daimler/Leyland Fleetline and MCW Metrobus the Ailsa B55 was a small player in the WMPTE operation but nonetheless a successful one, the early sale of the production batch being dictated by WMT's desire to standardise its fleet rather than by dissatisfaction with the type. Moreover, the transfer of a full batch of 50 production vehicles to another major operator in a commercial deal was probably unique, as was the ability of over 80% of the batch to find at least one further home after nearly 15 years' intensive use in two of the country's harshest operating environments. The early faith placed by Volvo in the development of the Ailsa B55 certainly proved to be well grounded.

Top: Most of the ex-WMPTE Ailsas saw further service after their spell in London, some even returning to the West Midlands, where they were bought by small operators. These latter included Tame Valley, for which the former 4740 is seen running in Birmingham city centre in February 1992.

Above: The end. The buildings give a clue that this is not the West Midlands but West Yorkshire. Keith Billingsley's preserved 4738 heads into Morley, working for Black Prince on that company's last day of operations, 30 July 2005.

Over fell and through dale

In 2008 **Tony Wilson** sampled some vintage hospitality in the Yorkshire Dales and the Pennine Moors.

All photographs by the author

DURING 2008 I again had the opportunity to sample some of our finest vintage buses still operating in revenue-earning service. Of course there are one or two well-known vintage operations in places like Blackpool and London, but the subjects of this photo-feature are to be found running through the Yorkshire Dales and the North Pennines.

I am fortunate enough to be associated with the Hamer family of Bowber Head, Ravenstonedale, near Kirkby Stephen, on the eastern fringes of Cumbria, for it is from this semi-remote location high up in the Fells that they run Cumbria Classic Coaches. The fleet currently consists of four single-deck and two double-deck vehicles, which range in age from 1946 to 1959. All are retained as near as possible in their former operators' liveries and are used throughout the year. However, from Easter to October the buses find regular work on seasonal stage services, and indeed 2008 marked the 10th anniversary of vintage-bus service 569 to and from Hawes, in Wensleydale. Another local operator to evoke nostalgia in 2008 was Chris Bulmer's Vintage Omnibus Services, which ran a trio of Bristol single-deckers — two half-cab L types and one underfloor-engined MW — on route 127 from Ripon.

Two events with vintage vehicles were organised in the area during 2008. On the Saturday and Sunday of the Easter weekend the 10th Kirkby Stephen Classic Commercial Vehicle Rally was held at Kirkby Stephen and Brough, the two sites being linked by a free service operated by a selection of vintage buses. The event was accompanied by snow, which, fortunately, failed to deter the many entrants and visitors. At the other end of the season, in September, a modest but well-organised vintage-bus running day was organised at Hawes, this time in glorious late-summer sunshine.

Cumbria Classic Coaches' former Florence Motors AEC Regal JTB 749 with Burlingham bodywork trundles along the A685 as it heads towards Kirkby Stephen at the start of its run down through Mallerstang to Hawes on Tuesday-only route 569. Guaranteed a connection for the Settle–Carlisle railway line at Kirkby Stephen West station, passengers sit back and enjoy the splendid scenery that both east Cumbria and the western Yorkshire Dales afford.

Right: In June 2008 a new route was inaugurated by Cumbria Classic Coaches, this being the Wednesday-only 572 from Ravenstonedale to Barnard Castle. Such had been the success of the route that it was extended through the winter months. However, contrasting with the situation in the summer, when the service operated over Stainmore Common and Lune Moor to Middleton-in-Teesdale and then Barnard Castle, during the more inclement months buses ran direct along the A66 to and from Brough. From day one the regular performer on the service was this former Crosville Bristol Lodekka, 627 HFM. Here the bus takes in its stride the long stiff climb up out of Brough over Stainmore Common and in so doing offers passengers a panoramic view back over the Eden Valley, here spread out behind the vehicle.

Left: At times the double-decker has been unavailable and to meet demand has been replaced by three single-deckers, as here. Resting between duties in the main car park at Barnard Castle are, from left to right, former Lancashire United Transport Guy Arab MTJ 84, the ex-Florence Motors AEC Regal and one-time Preston Corporation Leyland Tiger CRN 80.

Left: For several years Cumbria Classic Coaches has run a summer school-holiday contract in Kendal. This circular town-centre service provides a park-and-ride facility to try to reduce the number of cars making journeys into and out of the town. Subsidised by the burghers and shopkeepers of Kendal, the route was generally in the hands of this former Alexander Leyland Tiger, CWG 286. Here the bus stands for a few moments in the main shopping street before setting off on one of the 11 round-trips operated each day.

Left: In September 2008 Cumbria Classic Coaches provided one of its buses for a two-day event at Middleton-in-Teesdale, allowing visitors the opportunity to discover some of the more inaccessible areas on the fells above the town. Here the former Preston Corporation Leyland Tiger meanders through some rather bleak countryside.

Right: A Bristol L from Chris Bulmer's Vintage Omnibus Services operation, restored in full Lincolnshire Road Car livery, FFW 830 carries a near full load through the village of Redmire. It is heading westwards through Wensleydale on route 127 to Hawes, where on Tuesdays it linked up with Cumbria Classic Coaches' 569/570 service.

Left: Red Bristol half-cab LHN 823 in somewhat inclement conditions, which tended to be a symptom of the summer of 2008. However, many visitors to the area took the opportunity to ride in this vehicle, a former United Automobile L type.

Right: On occasions the service required more than one bus to transport customers. Returning to Ripon in the late afternoon on a bright and sunny day, ex-Eastern National Bristol MW 208 YVX is duplicated by the United L. The pair are seen approaching the village of Wensley — the only place where they headed into the sun, affording a photographic opportunity.

Left: One of the undoubted stars of the 10th Kirkby Stephen rally was this 1932 Sentinel DG4 32-seat steam bus, KG 1123. Brought up from Broughton-in-Furness, it performed on the main road between Brough and Kirkby Stephen several times on both days of the event. Here, with a good load of passengers sampling the wooden-slatted seating, it arrives back at the Brough terminus pursued by ex-London Routemaster RML2290.

Right: As 2008 drew to a close, the newest vehicle to join the fleet arrived in the shape of UTC 672, a former Bamber Bridge Motor Services AEC Regent III with lowbridge East Lancs bodywork. Here the bus poses in somewhat gloomy conditions in the depths of winter at the Wensleydale Creamery, a location perhaps best known for its association with television characters Wallace and Gromit.

Going Solo

Stephen Morris examines the history of the most successful model produced by Optare.

IT IS OFTEN CONSIDERED — and not without justification — that the low-floor revolution in Britain was due largely to the Dennis Dart SLF. Certainly that was one bus which made the move to low-floor affordable for operators, and meant that the UK was quickly ahead of the game in offering all passengers accessible buses. Overnight step-entrance buses became obsolete; low-floor double-deckers were quickly developed, and soon heavyweight low-floor single-deckers were commonplace.

But the Dart wasn't the only contender in the market for a smaller, lighter-weight low-floor bus. Whilst it has never come close to matching the Dart's remarkable success, Optare's Solo has nonetheless become a major contender in the low-floor market. Although by the time it was superseded by the very similar Enviro200 the Dart had achieved sales in excess of 12,000 (of which more than 9,000 were low-floor), the Solo had at the time of writing reached a respectable total of well over 3,000 and rivals the Dart for versatility.

At the upper end of its size range the Solo is effectively a head-to-head rival of the Dart, but its unusual style of having no front overhang and the door within the wheelbase means that smaller versions developed down the years have made it a suitable accessible replacement for the 'bread vans' of yore. Thus the Solo has become the low-floor successor to the true minibus, bringing accessibility to places which might otherwise not have been able to sustain low-floor buses.

In some ways the Solo takes Optare back to its roots. The company was formed when former plant director Russell Richardson bought the factory he had managed for Leyland Bus, that of Charles H. Roe

Launch customer for the Optare Solo was Wilts & Dorset, which ordered no fewer than 85 for delivery in 1998/9. An example of the original 8.5m-long, 2.5m-wide model leaves Salisbury bus station in the summer of 2006. MATTHEW WHARMBY

in Leeds, at a time when bus services were about to be deregulated. This was an audaciously brave move at a time when the market had totally collapsed as a result of uncertainty and when the perceived wisdom was to reduce capacity in the bus-building industry. The key to the company's survival was innovation, which it demonstrated with its first 'serious' model, the VW-based CityPacer 25-seat midibus, and there are clear hints of the CityPacer's ground-breaking styling in the Solo.

The CityPacer introduced Optare's new concept of being a 'one-stop shop'; whatever bus you bought was simply an Optare product, regardless of the chassis on which it was based. This was a radical way of selling buses: traditionally buyers bought a chassis from one company and a body from another and hoped nothing would go wrong with it in the 'grey area' in which both builders could claim the warranty responsibility was down to the other. It was, of course, a logical step for Optare to eliminate the separate chassis altogether, which it did when it acquired from MCW the rights to build the Metrorider — a complete, all-steel midibus, which it reworked and renamed very subtly as the MetroRider.

For its big buses — the DAF-based Delta, Mercedes-based Prisma, MAN-based Vecta and DAF-based Spectra double-decker — Optare had pioneered the UK use of the Swiss Alusuisse system of bolted aluminium construction, later to be used by other builders such as Wright and East Lancs. But the MetroRider's all-steel construction was to be the basis of its integral low-floor products and was adapted for its Excel single-decker, which spanned the gap between midibus and full-size single-decker. Again its styling was ground-breaking.

Unlike the front-engined MetroRider the Excel was rear-engined and used an innovative system of a cradle to contain the main mechanical units. This meant that the whole bus could be built before the really expensive bits had to be bought in, helping the company's cash flow, and that engine changes could be undertaken very easily, the self-sealing connectors used for the pipework meaning that you could pretty well slide a fork-lift under the engine and simply withdraw it.

Unfortunately the Excel proved not to be Optare's finest hour; it was a brave attempt, but although at the time of its introduction its styling was way ahead of other products on the market, it dated quickly, and there were numerous tales of mechanical unreliability. Its reworking as the Excel 2 came too late, and whilst operators of the improved model seemed much more satisfied, only a few were

prepared to take the chance. But it was obvious that there was still much demand for lighter-weight, smaller buses — and that demand for step-entrance buses had virtually ceased as soon as the first Dart SLF took to the road. What was wanted was a low-floor replacement for the MetroRider, and Optare drew up something that was in effect an amalgamation of Excel and MetroRider. So although the new product looked like a conventional front-engined midibus it wasn't: it was rear-engined, being very similar in concept to the Excel, complete with cradle-mounted power pack.

Whereas the Excel had employed Cummins' B-series six-cylinder engine, as used in the Dart but to a higher rate of tune, the Solo was to use the driveline of the bus it was really aimed at replacing — the Mercedes-Benz Vario. Thus it had the four-cylinder, 12-valve Mercedes OM904LA 122bhp engine, and where the Excel used Allison's high-tech World Series electronically-controlled automatic, which it needed to cope with the power and torque of the B-series at the top end of its settings, the Mercedes engine required only the much simpler (and more familiar) mechanically controlled AT545 gearbox.

At this time Mercedes-Benz was dominating the small-bus market, and the Vario had recently replaced the T2 range, of which the 709D and 811D were most popular as the basis for small buses. Indeed, Wright, it is understood, had developed a low-floor version of the Vario in conjunction with Mercedes, using a 'drop box' behind the gearbox to lower the propshaft at the front end, as well as a gently sloping floor to clear the normal Vario rear axle. This layout was already used by Wright to simplify low-floor design on vehicles like the Scania-based Axcess-ultralow. It all seemed straightforward — the required drop box was already used by Mercedes in military applications. But, much to Wright's chagrin, it never saw the light of day, and this left the market clear for the Solo.

However, having designed it, Optare was cautious about launching the Solo. One thing that had emerged in its research was that passengers didn't like sitting cheek-by-jowl on narrow minibuses, and as the Excel was already 2.5m wide it required less development to release the Solo at the same width. By then the overall width restriction had increased, quite suddenly, to 2.55m, and although new low-floor double-deckers, designed from scratch, would emerge at the same time as the Solo at 2.55m, the Solo was too far forward in its design cycle and remained at 2.5m. Two lengths were available, 8.5m and 9.2m, allowing up to 33 and 37 seats respectively.

One operator which had a large requirement for smaller buses and was already firmly committed to Optare as a supplier was Wilts & Dorset. At the time this privatised former NBC subsidiary was still (very) independent; its management team had its own particular ideas on running buses and seemed determined to carry on doing so. Ultimately Wilts & Dorset would surprise everyone by selling out in August 2003, although the group to which it sold, Go-Ahead, would be less of a surprise; of all the big groups it encouraged the most independent approaches in its subsidiaries. But in 1997, when Optare was developing the Solo, that was all several years away.

Wilts & Dorset had the biggest fleet of Spectras (it had 50 at the time) and relied heavily on MetroRiders, which appeared everywhere on its network. One sign of W&D's independence lay in the way its schedules were drawn up, such that small buses would appear anywhere at slacker times, and double-deckers on major routes when needed. Thus its MetroRiders were regarded as maids-of-all-work, sometimes appearing on lengthy trunk routes. However, Wilts & Dorset was among the operators wanting wider small buses and had quite a lot of input into Solo's design; indeed, it was W&D's willingness to order 85 off the drawing-board that convinced Optare to launch the model.

The first Solo was ready in time for Coach & Bus '97, where it appeared with a low-floor Spectra, Optare winning the race to deliver the UK's first low-floor double-deckers. Although the low-floor 'decker had been expected to be largely a London phenomenon, the first was a Spectra for ABus of Bristol, which stole Travel West Midlands' thunder by getting its bus into service a few hours before TWM's similar vehicle. However, at Coach & Bus '97 the Solo was rather overshadowed by the first Plaxton President. Based on a Volvo B7L chassis, with rear engine mounted longitudinally on the nearside, it turned out to be a white elephant, but nevertheless it was this bus that really heralded the era of the low-floor double-decker; the original, step-entrance Spectra had stolen the show in 1991, but, with no significant change when it evolved as a low-floor bus, the response to it was rather underwhelming.

In fact Optare had formally launched the Solo a few weeks before the 1997 show, the first appearing *inside* a Leeds hotel as part of the press launch. As well as the Mercedes engine it had Albion axles (similar to those on the Roadrunner truck but slightly wider) and air-over-hydraulic brakes all round. Another unusual feature was that instead of a conventional wiring loom it used car-style multiplex wiring, with a single ring main and sender units located around the vehicle which acted on pulses sent around the ring main to activate nearby electrical components. This reduced the complexity of the wiring and also gave additional diagnostic capability.

Having the door behind the front axle meant approach angles didn't have an impact on step height, and whereas the goal for most builders was to get down to a 300mm step height, the Solo was able to come in lower still, at just 250mm. Moreover there was no intrusion from the front wheel-arches, as these were within the cab area, so the saloon was remarkably uncluttered, and 70% of seats were at low-floor level. With its low build and full air suspension, the Solo gave a particularly good ride and indeed remains exceptional in this respect today.

Production began in January 1998, but by the time of the 1997 show Optare had been able to announce orders worth £9 million: in addition to Wilts & Dorset's 85, Travel West Midlands had ordered 30. Wilts & Dorset received its first batch of 11 by May 1998, introducing them on Poole local services, and over the summer famously made Salisbury the first all-low-floor city in Britain when it replaced its MetroRiders there with Solos and introduced low-floor Spectras to replace the double-deck fleet. Meanwhile Travel West Midlands increased its order, and other new volume customers included Go North East, Reading Buses, Nottingham City Transport and MK Metro. By the summer of 1998 some 300 had been ordered, and despite Optare's initial reluctance to put it into production the Solo had become its fastest-selling bus.

Although Optare had become known for supplying primarily medium-sized independent operators, like Wilts & Dorset, Trent and Reading Buses, the Solo was going to change all that. First of the big groups to buy any was First, which took 14 for PMT in 1999 followed by a batch for Manchester, ultimately building up a nationwide fleet of 200. Stagecoach took a little longer to fall for its charms but bought its first, for Leamington and Warwick, in 2001. From having bought next to no Optare products Stagecoach suddenly adopted the Solo as one of its standard models and including those taken over with other operators now runs nearly 700; the Preston Bus fleet, taken over in 2009, included some 70 Solos. Arriva has been less enthusiastic but now has around 100 in the UK plus seven left-hand-drive examples in service in Denmark. However, it was at the other end of the scale that the Solo really scored. It was made available through dealer Mistral, which rents, leases and sells buses, and this more than

Export markets were explored, though few Solos were actually exported. An American version built by NABI sold in respectable numbers, mainly to smaller operators and to airlines and car-hire firms.
STEPHEN MORRIS

anything has attracted smaller operators which wouldn't normally buy Optare products. Thus Solos can be found in independent fleets throughout the country, and not merely in penny numbers. Brylaine, of Boston, to take one at random, has had no fewer than 28, while Courtney of Bracknell has 35. The type has also proved popular amongst local authorities.

Following acquisition by North American Bus Industries, which despite its name was a Hungarian company (albeit with much of its capital based in Jersey), Optare made the Solo available in the USA as the NABI 30LF. In place of the Mercedes engine was the Cummins B series, and 75 were ordered by American Eagle Airlines.

In 2004 came major extensions to the Solo range. The Mercedes engine was adequate for the Vario, but the largest Solos found themselves rather short on power, even with an uprated,145bhp unit, so Optare offered the Cummins ISBe engine, the Euro3 version of the B series. In most comparable buses the 3.9-litre four-cylinder ISBe has sufficed, but to bring more power and refinement to the Solo the bigger, six-cylinder variant was offered, rated at 185bhp and necessitating a 300mm extension to the rear overhang in order to accommodate it. Transmission was standardised on the larger Allison 2000 five-

speed unit, which had been available as an option. At the same time a new interior was introduced, based on that of the Excel 2 and featuring rather neat concealed lighting. But perhaps the most significant addition to the range was something that had been lacking from the start — a narrower, SlimLine version, just 2.33m wide. There was also an extended model, with an overall length of 9.9m, which increased to 10.2m with the Cummins engine. Cooks Travel, later taken over by Stagecoach, was the first user of the new model, on an Exeter park-and-ride service. Shortly afterwards it was announced that a 7.8m version of the SlimLine would be available, making the Solo into a true low-floor minibus, which would get even smaller with the announcement in 2006 of the 7.1m, 24-seat SE model. With a wide range now available the Solo was selling more strongly than ever, and additional capacity was made available at Optare's Rotherham plant in order to cope with demand.

Almost a sideshow was the development of a hybrid model. The diesel-electric hybrid was becoming something of a holy grail, and despite working well in the USA was proving elusive in Britain. Although Optare itself wasn't at this stage interested in developing a hybrid bus it supplied a number of rolling shells to Eneco, which was developing a hybrid system using a VW 1.9-litre engine and generator. One unit was fitted to an existing First Manchester bus, while others were supplied as new buses to Ipswich Buses and Merseyside PTE. Unfortunately not enough

Above: Although the Solo was offered initially to a standard width available in just two lengths, the range was increased considerably in 2004, when longer, shorter and narrower versions were introduced. This view features the original 2.5m-wide version (right) alongside the 2.33m SlimLine.
STEPHEN MORRIS

Right: The Solo took Optare into new markets, especially amongst independent operators like Tyrer Bus of Nelson, which took three SlimLines in 2006. One is seen leaving Burnley bus station.
STEWART J. BROWN

Left: The Solo also took Optare into the big groups. Some of the earliest examples for First were for service in Manchester.
STEPHEN MORRIS

Above: After a slow start Stagecoach adopted the Solo as a standard type and now runs about 700. Working for Stagecoach North West, this one is seen in Preston bus station in 2007. STEWART J. BROWN

Below: Arriva's Solos include SlimLine models, ideal for services which operate in confined spaces such as this supermarket car park in Salford. STEWART J. BROWN

Above: Eneco's prototype hybrid bus. The Eneco-powered Solo proved to be a disappointment.
STEPHEN MORRIS

Right: First Manchester had this Solo converted from diesel power as one of the Eneco hybrid prototypes. It was used on the free MetroShuttle service in central Manchester.
STEPHEN MORRIS

Right: The Solo has proved popular with local authorities. This 7.8m SE, seen in 2005 in the then-new Norwich bus station, was used by Norfolk County Services on the short-lived Norwich Orbital service.
STEPHEN MORRIS

Below: Cook's Coaches was the first customer for the longest version, for use on the Exeter Park & Ride service. Its 9.9m length — that's 32ft 6in — is apparent in this view and is in sharp contrast to the compact dimensions of the 7.8m SE.
STEPHEN MORRIS

Right: A recent spin-off of the Solo is the Versa, which has been popular with Transdev. This is one of Lancashire United's, used on Blackburn local services but here hosting a Bus Users UK 'bus user surgery' in the town.
STEPHEN MORRIS

development had gone into it, and the project came to nothing. When they did work the buses proved noisier and less fuel-efficient than straightforward diesels, which wasn't quite the object of the exercise. At least with Optare's cradle mounting for the power pack it was a comparatively simple matter to convert them to conventional buses.

Meanwhile another option was offered with the move to Euro4 engines, which needed some form of exhaust after-treatment to meet the tougher new emissions limits. Two principal methods were used. One, Exhaust Gas Recirculation (EGR), involved reintroducing some of the exhaust gas into the cylinder to complete the combustion and to lower engine temperatures, though the drop in combustion temperature increased the particulate emissions and therefore needed a particulate filter. The other method was to increase combustion temperature to ensure particulates were fully burned up and to deal with the resulting nitrogen oxides by injecting a small amount of urea solution into the exhaust ahead of the catalytic converter, a process known as Selective Catalytic Reduction (SCR). Different manufacturers opted for different solutions, and both the Mercedes and Cummins engines used SCR, though the Mercedes was running at Euro5 levels as a result. However, in order to appeal to operators who didn't want the hassle of having to top up the

vehicle with the Adblue urea solution Optare turned to MAN for its EGR D0834 four-cylinder 4.6-litre 177bhp engine as an additional option.

Despite having been around for nearly 10 years it was now time for the Solo to spawn new models. Most radical was the Versa, announced at the 2006 Show. A stylish 10.3 or 11m bus with 36-40 seats, the Versa abandoned the Solo's basic concept of lacking a front overhang, instead having a conventional front platform and more rounded styling, incorporating slightly curved glass to cut down what was described as 'flutter', the way flat glass can shake, particularly when the bus is idling. Some of the first entered service at the end of 2007 with Stagecoach, which took the first 25, and with Arriva, and the model has also been well received by Transdev, a new customer for Optare, which is running examples in Blackburn, Bournemouth and London.

The most radical facelift of the Solo itself came with the launch of the SR model for the 2007 Coach & Bus show. This was available as a top-of-the-range vehicle, recognising a move amongst some operators to take buses further up-market, and incorporated some of the features of the Versa, including the

The first examples of the Solo SR to enter service were eight delivered to Preston Bus in May 2008 to upgrade the city's Park & Ride service. They had leather seats. STEWART J. BROWN

curved side windows. So far not many have been sold, but the Solo SR entered service with Preston Bus prior to the latter's takeover by Stagecoach and is also operated by Lothian and by Arriva in Derby and Tunbridge Wells, as well as by the Atomic Weapons Establishment at Aldermaston.

As if all this were not enough another new Solo model appeared at EuroBus Expo 2008 in Birmingham. By now Optare had merged with Darwen Group, owner of East Lancs, which wasted no time in developing a new double-deck model, the Rapta, and a revised Solo, the Solo Plus. This would be available in diesel, hybrid or battery-electric form. However, where Optare had been making subtle use of curves to create a stylish appearance and had been moving the interior upmarket, the Solo Plus reversed both trends with almost brutal styling and a much more basic interior. Unusually for any product — and especially so for one with Optare's name on it — the Solo Plus was received by the trade press with universal opprobrium, and the company will not be proceeding with this version in the form in which it was launched.

For a model that was launched so tentatively back in 1997 the Solo has been remarkably successful. From Optare's usual customer base of medium-sized operators it has spread throughout the market to become a familiar sight throughout Britain, proving itself a capable performer on all kinds of duties.

Moreover, from having options only of two lengths, it now encompasses a range of lengths from 7.1 to 10.2m in widths of 2.33m or 2.5m (depending on length) and with seating capacity ranging from 23 to 37, while engines, from Mercedes, Cummins and MAN, range from 127bhp to 201bhp. There is also the upmarket SR, available in lengths of 8.9m and 9.6m and widths of 2.4m and 2.5m. Thus, whilst remaining true to its name by virtue of its class-beating low step, in terms of its wide range the Solo now represents a sizeable ensemble.

Solo and Versa variants 2009

Model	Length	Width	Seats	Notes
M710SE	7.1m	2.33m	23	
M780SE	7.8m	2.33m	24	
M810	8.1m	2.33m	24	
M880	8.8m	2.33/2.5m	29	
M890	8.9m	2.4/2.5m	29	Solo SR
M950	9.5m	2.33/2.5m	33	
M960	9.6m	2.4/2.5m	33	Solo SR
M1020	10.2m	2.5m	37	
V1040	10.4m	2.5m	36	Versa
V1110	11.1m	2.5m	40	Versa

The heyday of half-cabs at Maidstone & District

Michael H. C. Baker flicks through the pages of a 1950 'ABC' of Maidstone & District and recalls the great days of the company's half-cab coaches.

All photographs by the author or from the author's collection

THE IAN ALLAN Maidstone & District 'ABC' of 1950 lists 232 coaches among a total fleet of 850 — a great contrast with today, when coaches hardly figure at all in many large fleets. All had been built between 1930 and 1949, and all were based on Leyland Tiger or AEC Regal chassis with the exception of 12 normal-control Dodge coaches new in 1940/1.

Just why did the company need so many coaches? In 1950 petrol rationing was still in force, television was in its infancy, there was virtually no unemployment as the country got down to repairing the ravages of war and people were relatively well-off. Which meant they had money to spend on travel.

The Kent and Sussex coasts can probably boast more resorts, large and small, than anywhere else in England, all within easy reach of London and therefore popular with day excursionists. Unfortunately for Maidstone & District practically all of the direct coastal services to and from London's Victoria Coach Station were the preserve of either East Kent or Southdown, leaving M&D with just two North Kent routes, Faversham and Sheerness, and three to East Sussex, serving Rye, Bexhill and Hastings. These five were all-year-round services. Other summer-only operations linked the Medway towns, Dartford, Gravesend and Maidstone with Margate, Folkestone, Hastings, Eastbourne, Brighton, Portsmouth and Southsea. Yet neighbouring East Kent, connecting London Victoria with Herne Bay, Whitstable, Ramsgate, Broadstairs, Margate, Deal,

Walmer, Sandwich, Dover, Folkestone and Hythe, could boast only 118 coaches. Southdown, serving Eastbourne, Seaford, Newhaven, Brighton (which at times generated almost as much business as any six of the others put together), Hove, Worthing, Littlehampton, Bognor Regis, Hayling Island, Southsea, Portsmouth and Gosport, owned 335 coaches.

The cover of Ian Allan's 1950 *ABC of Maidstone & District* featured what was at the time a modern coach, showing one of the last five 1949 Regal IIIs, which had full-fronted Harrington bodies, rather than a more typical half-cab coach.

Yet despite being squeezed out of so much of the lucrative traffic between Central London and the seaside, well over a quarter of Maidstone & District's fleet was composed of coaches. Let the 'ABC' — which is not credited to any particular author but was 'produced in collaboration with' the company — explain. 'An important feature of the Company's activities to-day is the Private Hire Department, which provides a comprehensive service for its clients by booking tickets for theatres and sporting events, arranging catering facilities, and even coach/air trips to the Continent. A particular feature of the work undertaken is organising trips which last a number of days — a typical example of which is the tour made by the Australian Women's Cricket Team when they visited this country. A specially fitted coach was placed at their disposal for the duration of their visit and upon another occasion an M&D coach has been hired to take a wedding party to Scotland.' There were, it continued, 'coach/air trips to the Continent', while 'finally, mention should be made of the all day and part day excursions which operate from all depots, particularly during the summer season. Kent and Sussex are rich in scenic beauty and historical associations and trips to these places are extremely popular among holiday makers in the Garden of England.'

Another rich source of income for the coaching fleet was Chatham Naval Base, for long one of the principal homes of the British Navy. Although by 1950 relatively few National Servicemen were being called into the Navy, leave specials were big business, whilst the 10,000 civilian employees were great patrons of public transport. HMS *Victory* was built at Chatham, as were successive generations of battleships until 1914, and although the dockyard would eventually close in 1984, 30 years earlier it was still a vital part of the country's naval operation and its principal submarine base.

In the other direction visitors to the Medway towns were attracted by the Charles Dickens connection, so many of his stories being set in and around there and on the Thames Estuary. His father, John, was pay clerk in Chatham Dockyard between 1817 and 1823, and from 1857 until his death in 1870 Dickens lived at Gads Hill, just outside Rochester. No doubt in a more publicity-conscious age Maidstone & District would have named its coaches after characters from his stories.

What of the vehicles? Although the chassis of many of the coaches dated back to 1930 these had all been rebodied later in the decade, or even postwar. Almost all were by Harrington, the exceptions being 30 postwar bodies by Beadle and the 12 Dodges

dating from 1940/1, which had Duple bodywork very like that fitted to the Bedford OB. Indeed these were, apparently, meant to be Bedfords with particularly luxurious 24-seat bodies for touring, but the order was transferred to Dodge on account of war restrictions, this Kew-based firm of American origin being a most unusual supplier of buses or coaches to a BET company, or, indeed, to anyone else. (One has to wonder just why, at the start of the war, the order went ahead at all.) The 30 postwar Beadle bodies closely resembled the Harringtons, so that the Maidstone & District coach fleet presented a remarkably uniform appearance, the mid-1930s bodies being very little different from the postwar versions. And what a splendid-looking fleet it was.

Harrington coach bodies of the mid- and late 1930s marked perhaps the high-point of half-cab coach design. Their flowing lines, tipping slightly downwards at the front and rear with elegant curves above the side windows and the front destination indicator (not that there was one at the back), lacked any ornamentation apart from a flash sweeping down midway from beneath the windows to behind the rear wheel-arch. The livery of dark green below and cream above, with that superb bold gold lettering inside a scroll, suited the design to perfection. This was reversed at the end of 1948, cream becoming the main colour below the waistline, and perhaps this was even better.

Throughout the 1920s Maidstone & District had been one of the best customers of the local firm of Tilling-Stevens, but the arrival of the Leyland Tiger and the AEC Regal brought the relationship to a shuddering halt. In 1950 there were 29 elderly Regal coaches dating from 1930-3 but with bodies built 1937-9, apart from three fitted in 1946. All had petrol engines. Normally Maidstone & District vehicles were allocated Kent registrations, but 10 of the Regals had been acquired from Timpsons in 1934 and had DY (Hastings) registrations. They originally had Harrington bus bodies but were given new coach bodies just before the outbreak of war.

The rest of the prewar coaches were Tigers — 42 TS7s, dating from 1935/6, and 33 TS2s. Thirty of the TS2s, built in 1930, had bodies of 1937/8 vintage, the final three, dating from 1931, being given new bodies as late as 1946. By 1950 there were many gaps in the prewar coach fleet, some of the Tigers having passed to London Transport and worked briefly as Green Line coaches, whilst many more were requisitioned for war service and never returned to the fleet. From 1946 coaches with diesel engines were given a 'CO' prefix ('O' for oil), and from 1950 the remaining petrol-engined vehicles were classed 'CP'.

Above: A 1939 view in Maidstone of a 1936 Leyland Tiger TS7 with original Harrington body, showing the original coach livery with green lower panels. This coach was rebodied in 1950 and operated for M&D until 1958.

Below: Prominent in this prewar view is an ex-Timpsons AEC Reliance, new in 1929 and rebodied by Harrington in 1936. When it was withdrawn in 1949 the body, then 13 years old, was transferred to a new AEC Regal III chassis; that coach was in turn withdrawn in 1955, its mechanical units being incorporated in a 'new' Beadle-built coach.

After the war AEC found itself back in favour, and the final half-cabs were all Regals. A new series of fleet numbers was started with CO1, which arrived in April 1947. It was a 32-seater, this being the M&D standard, and was the first of 31, the last arriving in March 1948. At around this time Southdown, another very good customer of Harrington, bought some rather curvaceous, rather florid-looking bodies from the Hove firm, but M&D's were quite different, scarcely distinguishable from the prewar Harrington design except that they had luggage racks at the rear of the roof; this was a rather old-fashioned feature, but they still looked very fine. Deliveries continued with 26 almost identical Beadle-bodied coaches, CO32-57, the last arriving around Christmas 1948. These were immediately preceded by the first of a fleet of Mk III Regals, once again with Harrington bodies, but this time without roof-mounted luggage accommodation. The bodies on 23 of these coaches actually dated from 1936, having been transferred from withdrawn AEC Reliances of 1929. The fact that 1936 bodies, refurbished by Portsmouth Aviation, could be mounted on 1948 chassis and look no different from bodies 12 years newer illustrates the timelessness of the mid-1930s design. The Regal IIIs were numbered CO62-112, the first arriving in March 1948, the last in December 1949. The final few arrived in the revised livery, and all

Maidstone & District coaches soon followed suit; how splendid they looked.

This in a sense ends the story of the half-cab coaches, but there is a postscript ... well, two actually. The last five Harrington-bodied Regal IIIs brought the tradition of elegance to an abrupt halt. They had full fronts and a plethora of side windows. If they were supposed to point to the future they actually looked old-fashioned, rather in the manner of those mid-1930s attempts at streamlining which didn't work. The Regals' successors were 72 more full-fronted Beadle coaches. Taking up work between August 1950 and early 1952, they had vertical engines, taken, along with the running units, from prewar AECs. From the front they bore some resemblance to the full-fronted Regals but were generally much better proportioned. Their lives as coaches were, however, very short, because in the spring of 1952 arrived the first underfloor-engined

Below: The close resemblance of the 1950 Harrington body to its prewar counterpart is apparent from this view of rebodied Tiger TS7 of 1936. Obvious differences include the absence of a roof-mounted luggage rack and the design of the sliding door, now opening on the outside of the body. Pictured in Victoria Coach Station in April 1955, ready to work a journey on the E5 service to Faversham, this coach would be withdrawn in 1958.

**Above: The first of the Beadle-bodied AEC Regals of
1948, seen on layover in London in 1955. The Beadle
body closely resembled those built by Harrington
for Maidstone & District. This coach was withdrawn
in 1959.**

**Below: A 1948 Harrington-bodied Regal III
in original livery.**

Above: A later view of a 1949 Regal, in the revised livery with cream lower panels.

Below: In the period 1950-2 prewar AEC running units were used by Beadle to create 'new' coaches for M&D. There were 72 such rebuilds, which wore this predominantly cream livery from new.

Above: A new generation of underfloor-engined coaches rendered half-cabs obsolete. This all-Leyland Royal Tiger joined the M&D fleet in 1952 and was operated until 1964. It is seen in Ramsgate in 1954.

Left: A modern mid-engined coach illustrates this mid-1950s fares leaflet, which reveals that the normal return fare from Hastings to London was 13s 3d (66p) but that at peak travelling times this increased to 15s 6d (77p), a hefty 17% premium.

LONDON by Coach
from HASTINGS
DAILY EXCEPT AS SHOWN BELOW

Day Return	8/9	Period Return	13/3

Whit-Saturday, Sunday & Monday and on Saturdays, Sundays and Bank Holidays, thereafter until the 30th September, inclusive.

Day Return	10/3	Period Return	15/6

THE Maidstone & District
MOTOR SERVICES LTD.

1, 3 & 5, PALACE AVENUE and
Coach Station, Central Cricket Ground
Telephone: HASTINGS 2310

coaches (Leyland Royal Tigers, shortly to be followed by AEC Reliances), which instantly rendered them out of date, and they ended their days as buses. However, although rapidly superseded by underfloor-engined designs — none of which could match the Harrington half-cab bodies for style until the superb, final flourish of Harrington Cavalier-bodied Reliances in the early 1960s — the 1936/7-vintage Tigers and the postwar Regals could on summer weekends throughout the 1950s be found in and around Victoria Coach Station, having worked up from Kent and Sussex. Clearly the company still took considerable pride in them, for they always looked immaculate.

Although the Tigers and Regals of the early 1930s had all gone by the early 1950s some of the rebodied TS7s had extraordinarily long lives. Three of the 1936 coaches were not withdrawn until 1962, whilst two from 1937 survived until 1964. Such was their longevity that they outlived all the Beadle rebuilds and all but two of the postwar Regals, which went at the same time. By this time bus and coach preservation by private individuals was well established, and both evaded the scrap dealer.

One has been a familiar sight at rallies ever since I first saw it, looking a bit sad, on tow at Penshurst in 1968; nowadays fully restored, it looks superb in the predominantly green livery it wore back in the late 1940s, a splendid reminder of the heyday of the Maidstone & District half-cab coach.

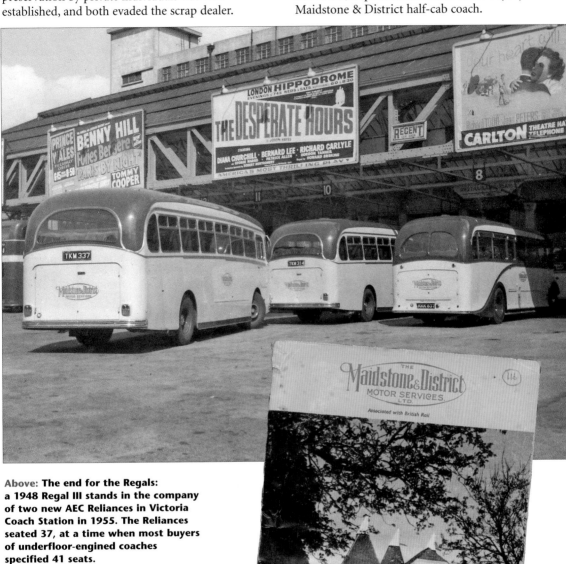

Above: The end for the Regals: a 1948 Regal III stands in the company of two new AEC Reliances in Victoria Coach Station in 1955. The Reliances seated 37, at a time when most buyers of underfloor-engined coaches specified 41 seats.

Right: Maidstone & District's timetable booklet played on Kent's fame as the Garden of England, this rural idyll being depicted on the cover of the 1966 edition. By this time the half-cabs had gone, but the image is redolent of 1950s Britain, where the sun always shone.

Buses at the top of the world

Greenland is a place seldom visited by transport enthusiasts. Tony Greaves made the trip.

All photographs by the author

GREENLAND'S LANDSCAPE is beautiful and at the same time hostile, and with its craggy volcanic mountains it appears an alien one. Our cruise visited the coastal settlements of Qoqortoq and Illulisat (they are merely that, because each is isolated, there being no internal road system, and travel is by ferry), but I was looking forward to landing at Nuuk, which held the possibility of interesting transport.

Many aboard ship doubted that we would reach Nuuk, for it is located in a rocky bay with many icebergs and 'growlers' (small icebergs), making it notoriously difficult for cruise ships to navigate. Indeed, one of the ship's entertainers said that he had been on 11 previous voyages with supposed landings at Nuuk and had not yet managed one! But the weather was good, and we landed by ship's tender.

Reykjavik is often hailed as the world's most northerly capital city (64°8' N), but, being located about 150 miles south of the Arctic Circle, at 64°10' N, the capital of the world's largest island takes the title by just two minutes. The city is commonly known as Godthåb (Good Hope) in Danish, although since home rule was enacted in 1979 it has been known officially by its Greenlandic name of Nuuk. Seat of government for the Sermersooq region, it has a population of just over 15,000, making it also one of the world's smallest capitals.

Local transport operator Nuup Bussii was founded in 1980 by the Nuup Kommunea (Municipality of Nuuk), has 24 employees, and its small fleet of buses travels 405,000 miles each year. Normal operating hours are quoted as 6.25am to 12.05am, 365 days a year. So this is the place for a bus ride on Christmas Day! At the time of my visit the fleet comprised 12 buses (since reduced to 10) of three distinct types — DAB/Silkeborg, Volvo B10M/Säffle and Volvo B12M with rather handsome Aabenraa (or Swedish Säffle) bodywork. Common to all was a standard internal layout which was surprisingly different from that found in the UK — not so much in terms of the four steps up into the saloon, nor of the 15 single seats on either side of the gangway, but the four steps down to a lowered rear platform for use by buggies and wheelchairs.

The fleet is very well kept, and apart from rust showing on the bumpers of the 1995 DABs the fleet was pristine, even sporting stainless-steel wheeltrims.

The fleet list, published on the internet by the operator (www.bus.gl), was a little confusing at first, and I initially fell into the trap of identifying all examples of a particular style of body as a Swedish Säffle. (It didn't help that none of them had a bodybuilder's badge or plate.) Closer examination of my photographs revealed detail differences in panel joins, size and style of grilles, so the conclusion is that the newer B12Ms are indeed bodied by Säffle but to the same design as the original Aabenraa. This is dual-sourcing, much like the near-identical bodies by Park Royal and MCW on London's DM/DMS-class Fleetlines but in some respects on a grander scale, the bodies in question coming from two different countries.

On my travels I relied mostly on multi-journey tickets cancelled on each journey by a machine which removes a small portion, although there is also an Ultimate-based system for individual journeys. There are five routes — 2, an 18-stop circular which takes 29 minutes to complete, X2 (a variation of the 2), E2 (a faster variation) and 3 and X3, which are more circulars. Nuuk is laid out as a grid, so the impression given is of constant high levels of traffic, but in truth the same vehicles are seen repeatedly — there is nowhere else for them to go as the roads cease not far beyond the edge of the city. Route 2 operates on a 15-minute frequency, but most of the other services are hourly. Bus shelters are large corrugated-metal affairs set on a concrete base (as are most of the buildings) and doubling as community notice boards.

A visit to Greenland is highly recommended, although anyone contemplating a cruise is advised to check that it goes as far as Disko Bay (yes, really), which is well to the north of the Arctic Circle; many tour operators who claim to visit the country reach only the southern tip. Having made the effort you will be rewarded with the sight of whales, icebergs, glaciers and breathtaking sheer mountains. And where else can you ride on a brand-new Volvo B12M dual-door bus?

Above: One of the oldest buses in the fleet at the time of the author's visit, a DAB which has since been withdrawn.

Below: This Säffle-bodied Volvo shows the two-door layout used by Nuup Bussii, with the exit in the rear overhang. It was new in 2008.

The last of the Aabenraa-bodied Volvo B12Ms, delivered in 2004, has just passed through the only traffic-light-controlled junction in Greenland. Aabenraa took its name from the Danish town where the company was based.

Above: This 1995 Volvo-powered DAB is now the oldest bus in the fleet. The bright-red box visible on the driver's right is the ticket-canceller.

Below: The city centre, where on-street buying and selling is going on in the background. This view of an Aabenraa-bodied B12M shows how Greenland retains the Danish practice of having a weights & measures panel on each side of the bus, with dimensions and seating/standing capacities included.

Time exposure

Gavin Booth considers the development of photography, from Kodak Box Brownie to compact digital.

All photographs by the author

IT WAS THE WAITING that was worst. You took your eight bus photographs, waited until you had finished your film, rewound the spool, carefully removed it from the camera, making sure no light affected the film, licked the little bit of sticky paper (yes, really) to seal the film tightly and marched off to the nearest chemist, who would tell you to come back in a few days' time to collect your prints.

If you had told me then, in the mid-1950s, that one day I would have a camera that could take literally thousands of photos without the need to reload, and that would show me the photo a fraction of a second after I had taken it, and that I could immediately E-mail it to any part of the world, I would have been interested but very sceptical. And what would there be left for chemists to do?

Photography has been a popular hobby since 1900, when George Eastman introduced his first Kodak Brownie camera, but more than half a century later, in the 1950s, it hadn't moved on very much. The camera that I used to take my first faltering steps in bus photography was based largely on Eastman's 1900 original. My father's Kodak Box Brownie camera allowed me to take eight photos on 620-size film, and if you think that nowadays you might routinely use eight photos on just one bus, half a century ago you used your ration very cannily, and it could take a long time to get to the end of a spool. When they came back from the chemist's I would sometimes find last summer's holiday snaps at the start of the film, such was the reluctance to 'waste' film. And as a 1950s schoolboy there was always the cost element as a control, both of the film itself and of developing and printing.

But that was how it was when I first felt the need to photograph buses — and, indeed, trams, as I did manage a couple of not very good photos of Edinburgh Corporation trams in the last week they operated, in November 1956.

Looking back we all probably wish we had taken more and better photos at an earlier stage in our lives, to record on film the buses (yes, and trams) that we grew up with in our formative years. My photographic experience had been restricted to photos of my parents and sister, probably on a beach somewhere around Britain on a sunny day, and this was what Box Brownies were designed for, not moving tramcars on a dreich November day.

Younger readers should be aware that the aforementioned Brownie was by no means a sophisticated beast. It was a box that was not greatly removed from the most primitive pinhole cameras, which were literally boxes with a pinhole that would be uncovered to allow the light to reach the sensitive film. My Box Brownie — in reality my father's, but

Left: An early Box Brownie attempt to catch a moving Edinburgh tram a week before the last trams were withdrawn. The scratches indicate that the author hadn't realised the importance of storing negatives safely. But he was only 13 at the time ...

I quickly gained possession — opened at the back to allow the film to be threaded onto the simple spool mechanism inside, and a little winding handle was provided to allow you to advance the film, watching carefully for the numbers that were printed on the film's backing paper to appear in the small red window in the corner. There was a simple fixed lens and a button that exposed the film to the light for the predetermined time. So no controls over exposure or shutter speed, then. Or, indeed, anything.

You viewed your photo through a simple mirror mechanism that was not aligned to the lens, but for the sort of photo most people took on their Brownies that was fine. It was only after I had been disappointed by the missing tops of buses — or sides, if I had been daring and taken an upright photo — that I learned about making allowances for this and not cropping too tightly.

The shutter speed was whatever Kodak had decided, probably slow enough to cope with the seaside snaps that most people wanted. It was certainly not fast enough to deal with moving buses, as I discovered when I got some experimental shots back from the chemist. And it certainly wasn't good enough to cope with photos taken in poor weather. But then, why would people ever need to take photos of moving things, and take photos in wintertime?

Well, I did, for one, and was delighted when I discovered that Kodak made a film called Tri-X with a 400ASA speed, which allowed the odd moving shot in reasonable weather and some passable — but grainy — shots in the Scottish winter. Suddenly bus photography became an all-year-round pursuit.

You could, of course, take photos using cameras much more sophisticated than my Box Brownie. There were Rolleiflex and Leica cameras that produced stunning images, some on film similar to that which I was using, but the results were many, many times better. There was even the relatively new 35mm film that some daring souls were using as an alternative to larger-format film. It was always thought that the size of the negative was important, so big negatives from a precision camera like a Rolleiflex were what most serious photographers aspired to. My Brownie produced equally large negatives, but there the similarity ended.

I should have said that we are talking black-and-white photos here. You could buy colour negative and transparency film, but it was hugely expensive to buy and to process. If you were hoping to sell photos to newspapers or magazines these were invariably published in black-and-white, so colour, you convinced yourself, was an expensive and self-indulgent luxury. If black-and-white television was all we had at the time, why on earth should we need colour photos?

Of course, we were wrong. The bus photographers who had the foresight/wherewithal/equipment to take colour photos in the 1950s now have editors and authors beating a path to their doors to have the opportunity to illustrate that era in colour.

But for me black-and-white film and the Box Brownie would have to do. I got better at working within the constraints of the camera and managed to produce some half-decent images that I have been able to use over the years. And the biggest satisfaction was to get my first photos published, two of them in the same issue of *Buses Illustrated* in February 1961. This spurred me on to take photos with half an eye to publication, and while I deluged the editor, Alan Townsin, with prints, not all found their way into the magazine.

Even with the basic fixed lens it was possible to get some decent bus photos, and my photo count rose as

I progressed through my teens. Most photos were taken in my native Edinburgh, but family holidays provided a perfect opportunity to take photographs that today are valuable historic records. The last big outing for the Brownie was a family holiday based in Bournemouth in 1961, when I must have got through several rolls of 620 film.

Soon after I started working, I think around 1962, I splashed out on a better camera. I was beginning to get just a bit ashamed of the Box Brownie, and while Kodak had moved on to slightly snazzier cameras that looked more 1960s but were essentially repackaged Brownies, I aspired to something closer to the type of camera I saw other enthusiasts using. I had joined The Omnibus Society in 1958 and noticed that as well as the Brownies there were some more sophisticated-looking pieces of kit.

So I went to Boots — no Jessops then — and invested in a fixed-lens camera that looked good, sophisticated and modern but was still essentially a simple device, with few if any controls. And, worst of all, it was a half-frame camera, which meant that it was set up to take two separate photos on what would normally be one 620-size frame, which resulted in strangely small (46mm x 31mm) negatives that didn't, I soon discovered, enlarge awfully well. As a Scot I was particularly attracted by the prospect of twice as many photos from a roll of film, but it proved to be false economy.

The next stage was to move up to a more expensive camera, and for my 21st birthday, in 1964, my parents bought me a Kodak Retinette. Now I was

motoring. Although the Retinette wasn't a single-lens reflex camera and still had a fixed lens it was a good lens and took (full-frame) photos on 35mm film. There was some control over aperture, focus and shutter speed, and I loved that camera. With 36 exposures at my command — and a wage coming in — I was able to get a bit more adventurous and take a bit more time and trouble with my photos. Most were still in black-and-white, but I did venture cautiously into colour in 1966 and increasingly from 1972.

The Retinette, I now realise, was a bit of a classic, and it certainly allowed me more flexibility. Now moving buses were not a problem, and the quality of the lens was such that good decent-sized prints could be produced. Its only drawback was the need to guess exposures or use the time-consuming exposure meter. Thank heavens through-the-lens metering was about to burst onto the scene.

By the mid-1960s some of the photos appearing in *Buses Illustrated* were moving away from the traditional front/nearside or front/offside views and were photos of (gasp) *moving* buses, and street scenes, and views that showed a lot of countryside and not so much bus. There had been a group of railway photographers who had been pushing back the barriers for some time and producing pictures that defied all the accepted conventions. Now there were bus photographers doing the same thing — people like Tom Moore, whose urban black-and-white shots are still probably unsurpassed, and Tony Moyes, who had a wonderful feel for rural shots

Left: The half-frame Boots camera could produce some satisfactory results, but there was little control, and its main plus-point was that it didn't look like a Box Brownie. This is a Devon General 'Sea Dog' Leyland Atlantean/MCW open-topper at Torquay in 1962.

Right: Getting a bit more adventurous with early Retinette colour and a shot inside Eastern Counties' Norwich garage in August 1966 with a range of Bristol/ECW products on show.

Above: The Retinette coupled with Tri-X film encouraged experimentation with 'different' shots, like this queue of stoic Edinburghers waiting in St Andrew Square for a bus.

Above: Early colour with the Retinette, and a 1965 attempt to recreate an iconic shot. At the time the result seemed disappointing, but 40-odd years later ...

(as well, I suspect, as a great deal of patience) and produced classics, the best-remembered probably being his shots in deeply rural parts of Wales.

With a regular income and the opportunity to travel more widely I tried to emulate Messrs Moore and Moyes but soon realised that much of their skill lay in taking good photos that could be perfected in the darkroom. Handing a film into the chemist was never going to give me the same quality, and even though I was now getting my developing and printing done in specialist photographic shops it was clear that only I could produce the sort of prints I had in my mind. Years before I had tried printing photos in the school photographic club and realised that this was a process that required patience and precision, neither of which are qualities I would pretend to possess.

The answer, I quickly decided, was to concentrate on colour and, in particular, colour slides; this way I could argue that the photos are made in the camera and, if I get them right, need no further tweaking.

I had also in the late 1970s moved on to my first single-lens-reflex (SLR) camera. The photographic shop I favoured was run by a Canon dealer, who convinced me that this was what I wanted. Since then I have poured many thousands of pounds into Canon's coffers, buying better and better cameras, plus lenses and other accessories.

And it was the idea of changing lenses that had partly pushed me on to SLRs. There are purists in bus photography who argue that photos should never be taken with anything but the standard 50mm lens — and, indeed, that photos should always be front-three-quarters views with no reflections and little or no background. Now I am very happy for them and long may they continue to take them, but that's not really for me. Of course, I have taken and still take photos that are essentially good record shots, and for reference — or, frankly, in the absence of anything else — they are useful to have. But useful rather than satisfying.

I'm sure Tom Moore and Tony Moyes and the first-rate bus photographers who have followed in their wake would argue that there is great satisfaction in producing a really good photo, whether by design or chance, and while I would class myself as a competent jobbing bus photographer I would never pretend that I can match their standards (not consistently, at any rate) and am still in awe of the people who take the first-class photos that appear in *Buses* and other magazines.

The Canon SLR encouraged an initial burst of excitement as I experimented with telephoto and wide-angle lenses before realising that some of them were so distorted as to be, well, silly, and so I am more controlled with my use of extreme lenses these days.

And now I am wedded to digital photography. I have never been an innovator, instead waiting to hear from friends how they fare and (that Scot again) waiting for prices to drop to more realistic levels. For a while I ran 35mm and digital Canons side by side,

Left: There's something satisfying about a line of buses, and the sculpted Leyland St Helens-style fronts of these Western SMT Albion Lowlanders and Leyland Titan PD3s lent themselves to a low-angle treatment at Kilmarnock in May 1974.

Right: A wide-angle lens allowed photos in restricted spaces that would otherwise have been impossible. This is March 1979 at Eastern Scottish's new Livingston depot, with a Leyland Fleetline/ECW over the pits. No, mechanics have not got younger — it was an Open Day, but it's good to see that Health & Safety was to the fore 30 years ago.

using the digital for photos that were required for magazines, sometimes instantly. The ability to take, check and E-mail a photo within seconds is still difficult to take in and obviously a huge leap from the Box Brownie and the chemist's shop. As 35mm slide film became more difficult to source I found myself using the 'old' Canon less and less — a pity, because the EOS 1000FN was by far the best of the many Canon film cameras I have owned, being light and simple to use while producing first-class results.

These days my best opportunities to take what I would regard as really satisfying photos come on

holidays, often overseas, when I have the time to suss out the best vantage-points and the time (and, amazingly, patience) to wait for the right bus or tram to come along to complete the process.

But I also get a lot of enjoyment from having the time to travel a bus route on a bright sunny day, looking for the backgrounds that would make a good picture. Bus photographers will surely agree that the sheer weight of urban traffic, moving or parked, has made our hobby that bit more difficult, and there have been lengthy exchanges in the columns of *Buses* magazine about the over-zealous policemen and security guards who seem to believe that someone blatantly photographing a London bus in the West End is somehow more of a security threat than the hundreds of camera-toting and mobile phone-wielding tourists all around, photographing everything in sight.

In addition to my big Canon EOS digital SLR I have a little Canon Ixus in a pouch on the belt of my trousers, and sometimes, when I don't fancy carrying the big camera and the lenses around in their case, I use the Ixus; it may lack the controllability of the EOS, but it produces excellent results. And it is more discreet and somehow appears less threatening than an SLR. And in many ways it is the 21st-century equivalent of the Box Brownie — simple and easy to use: just point and shoot. Its advantage over early-20th-century technology lies in its size, being a mere fraction that of the Brownie, and in the number of photos you can take — hundreds, even thousands,

depending on the size of card or disk you use and the fineness of the settings you choose. And another great thing about digital photography is that you don't have to wait to finish a film before changing to a faster film; you simply press a button, and the ISO speed is changed for as many photos as you wish.

For the first half-century from the introduction of the first Brownie popular photography progressed slowly, but in the past half-century it has moved through such delights as the 1952 Brownie 127, the 1963 Instamatic and the 1966 Advanced Photo System to 35mm compacts and on to digital, to the point where everyone seems to have a compact digital camera or a camera-phone whenever anything happens.

I would never presume to tell readers how to take good bus photos, but my friend Mark Lyons, one of the newer generation of excellent bus photographers, is writing a book about bus photography, and digital in particular, which is to be published by Ian Allan, publishers of this Yearbook.

Today the idea of the Box Brownie seems incredibly primitive, which I suppose it was, but it probably got quite a few of us Bus Photographers Of A Certain Age off to a good start.

Deregulation Glasgow in October 1986, with competing buses — from right a Strathclyde Atlantean, a Central Ailsa and a Kelvin Metrobus, all with Alexander bodies — silhouetted on Glasgow Bridge.

Above: London buses always look good in sunshine against a blue sky. This is Surbiton in May 2002, with a London United MCW Metrobus on the 418.

Below: Even in poor weather you can achieve good results. This BTS Routemaster was recorded at Oxford Circus in a June 1994 downpour.

Above: A snatched opportunity in London in April 1977 — a Routemaster on the 11 seen from the upper deck of the preserved ST922, then running a service to Covent Garden.

Above right: A variation on the same theme — a GTL Dennis Dart/Plaxton Pointer at Pier Head, Liverpool, early in 2005.

Below: A higher angle allows a different view on things. This is Sheffield in July 1994, with a Mainline Leyland-DAB artic plus a colourful selection of other buses in the background.

Above: A London bus queue in May 1979, with a mix of Routemasters, Fleetlines and Metropolitans stuck in Aldwych.

Below: After crossing Waterloo Bridge in London in July 2002 the author was confronted by this scene in the Strand, prompting a snatched shot of a sight that was fast disappearing as more Routemaster routes were converted to low-floor buses.

Off the wall

The phrase which forms the title has been applied to the works of **Robert E. Jowitt**, who strays through a bus strike and a rock festival with a temporary halt in Southampton before continuing to Luxembourg and a fancy in Nancy.

A FEW WEEKS AGO I chanced upon an out-of-date copy of *Buses* and, browsing through its pages, I encountered therein a review by editor Alan Millar on the (then) latest edition of *Buses Yearbook*. In this, *inter alia*, Mr Millar made mention of (I cannot remember his exact words, but approximately …) 'the usual off-the-wall article by Robert E. Jowitt'.

Now I do not in the very least mind having bricks thrown at my style of writing, for I am well aware that, for as many people as deplore it, justifiably in their view, there is an equal or probably greater number who relish it. Nevertheless, I was not at all sure whether or no this was in fact a brickbat. The term 'off the wall', to the best of my knowledge, was one applied to shady auctioneers who, upon seeing they had only one likely but enthusiastic prospective purchaser, would proceed to take bids from someone behind him, or in fact from imagination and the back wall. I am pleased to believe, by the way, that this system is no longer practised in at least the more respectable of auction sales.

Later I discovered, while confiscating a copy of the *Beano* from my youngest son, that there is a page therein containing extremely silly or facile letters (but what else could you expect?) from the readers assembled under this very title 'Off the Wall'. This hardly enlightened me, as my work, whatever anyone may think of it, can surely hardly be compared to readers' letters in a comic, even so well-worn a hero of antiquity as the *Beano*. Or so I hope!

I may here mention that whether articles for *Buses Yearbook* be 'off the wall' or good sound sense, the editor likes them all to be assembled under his hand or on his desk on 1 January. In my case this means spending all the spring thinking over what topic I shall choose, asking the editor in June or July if whatever-it-may-be is suitable to his purposes, reminding him a couple of months later what the

All photographs by the author

agreed subject was, mentally composing it until December, then sending Christmas cards and all that bourgeois jollification, writing half the article, along with thankyou letters, from 27 to 31 December, attending the King Alfred, Winchester, Running Day on 1 January and then begging the editor to extend his deadline …

In the early part of the year of grace 2008 I thought I had this whole scenario under control. I had despatched (probably late) my epic on driving buses for the Isle of Wight Rock Festival for *Buses Yearbook 2009*, and a fine new plot was looming. A good friend of mine (who hereinafter will be described as 'GF' — though these are not in fact his initials) invited me, as a PSV driver, to join him and a bunch of heroes he was assembling from all over southern England, to go strike-breaking.

It is not, I feel, politically correct to say which bus company was on strike, nor where was the scene of the endeavour, save only that the bus station in question is regarded by some observers as, even at the best of times, the most depressing in England … but of course that description could apply to many … In this particular case the spot was rendered the more dire by a bunch of tough pickets of as evil a mien as you would go a very long way to avoid. At all events our brave team was housed overnight in a coaching hotel not too far from the scene, with dinner and as much as you could drink without risk of a hangover intruding on the morrow's performance and a passably comfortable bed all at the expense of the leading lights of the strike-breakers. Dinner concluded with instructions, maps and timetables to each individual driver.

I counted myself fortunate that my duty started some two turns after that of GF, who was working on the same route as that for which I was booked, so I was able to travel with him and see how to drive an ultra-modern bus of which I had no previous experience and learn to operate a Wayfarer ticket-machine. So far so good. When it came to my turn to go out, however, first of all no decent modern bus could be found — obviously they had all gone out already — so I was presented, after some delay, with a totally unfamiliar and rather deplorable specimen, and then bidden to depart as of that moment at a time which bore no relation to the timetable.

The annual King Alfred Running Day in Winchester attracts enthusiasts and buses (albeit not many of King Alfred origin). On the left is a Plaxton-bodied Leyland Leopard restored in National Bus Company 'local coach' livery with Bristol fleetnames. The bus on the right is a former Crosville AEC Regal with Strachans body.

The result was that I spent the next two or three trips (or probably in fact two-and-a-half, for, empty, I was recalled by radio on the third) leap-frogging with other buses on the route. Meanwhile, brought up on Setright or at worst Almex ticket machines, I found myself completely at sea with the Wayfarer. When I was in the bus station an inspector operated the wretched machine for me. Otherwise, and *en route*, I fear, my records will have proved sadly adrift! With the end of my first session I decided enough was enough. My next schedule would be in falling darkness and night, and I was already counting myself lucky not to have either wrecked the bus or run down some harmless citizen, neither of which themes would have improved the strike-breakers' lot.

With words of explanation and apology to all those most concerned I abandoned the scene … Thus what might have proved an exciting article for *Buses Yearbook* descends to bathos, in a couple of (albeit lengthy) paragraphs plus a brief epilogue to complete the affair.

Not enough for *Buses Yearbook*! So whither? Some of the faithful among my readers may have spotted the fact that sometimes I indulge in the habit of penning a Second Part about a subject on which, even if two or three years previously, I have written already … 'off the wall' as may be!

The obvious is further experiences of the Isle of Wight Rock Festival, where I am bidden to turn up as driver in June 2008. This notion collapses when Go-Ahead Group, which now controls Southern Vectis and thus Rock-Festi buses, decides not to employ alien drivers, only denizens of its own companies. This may be because it has reason to believe that whoever rolled a white stone along the side of a Volvo (see last year's *Yearbook* article) may have been an alien … So in such circumstances I simply stray round the site taking photographs and hoping the powers will be in such straits as they might at the last moment demand my presence, which actually doesn't happen, and they don't.

Then how about Southampton? I have written of Southampton before; I not infrequently catch buses out of it, the more so these days when a kindly government grants me my senility and a free bus pass. Moreover it has a not uninteresting selection of buses, including, if you are lucky, an old Solent Blue Line with an Isle of Wight (DL) registration … too lengthy an affair to describe to anyone who does not understand. In fact, were I even to embark on this explanation I find I have little heart to describe Southampton these days. Since the Corporation Atlanteans have ceded the streets to the 'Barbie'

Above: In passing through Southampton in the spring of 2008 the author encountered, beside the historic Bargate, a thoroughly off-the-wall item ... and, yes, the numberplate is miraculously unoccluded, revealing that this MCW Metrobus once operated for West Midlands Travel. It was one of a batch of 50 delivered in 1986. And the author resisted the temptation to try the perfect snack!

Below: In the Southampton of 2008 Barbie is prominent ... but archetypal true love prevails. The buses are 1998 Northern Counties-bodied Volvo Olympians which had originally been operated by London Central.

Above: Better times in Southampton? This is a 1983 view, when Southampton City Transport's fleet consisted almost entirely of Leyland Atlanteans with East Lancs bodies. At the front is a 1971 bus, one of 25 delivered that year.

colours and the articulateds have torn their undersides off on the humps in Shirley and gone elsewhere the inspiration is lacking to write a follow-up article about the place … except I might mention a 'Temporay' (*sic*) bus stop which survived several weeks and even after receiving a 'spell-check' lasted quite a while longer. But as in the case of the Rock-Festi, one or two photos are all I feel up to supplying.

Inspiration has in fact been germinating, without my truly realising it, since before the notions of strike or the repeat of rock took hold, and perhaps Southampton's absent 'bendy-buses' proved a seed …

Some years ago I achieved an article on articulated buses … and this, given present trends in the bus industry, is plainly a topic — after failure of strike and rock — which I might usefully re-attack … Furthermore I have risked rash promises in these pages of what I would do in pursuit of such aims, as, for example, seeking the mega-bus — or three-part-articulated ex-Paris bus — in Bordeaux. Alas, I have failed to visit Bordeaux, and I fear that if I tried now it would prove far too late!

Nevertheless, despite the (presumed) demise of the Bordeaux mega-bus, I had my eyes on other developments in the articulated field.

Part of this was inspired as follows. I have a very dear friend in Luxembourg; I shall describe her hereinafter by the initials 'SP'. (These — as in the case of GF above — are not actually her initials, but if ever she should chance to read these passages she will be amused at this form of anonymity.) By profession she is a translator of learned books and political documents, but at other times she acts as a psychiatrist, with, I believe, considerable qualifications and quality. As such she sorts out my problems in return for my tidying her cellar. Furthermore she allows me her balcony to view a constant parade of Luxembourg buses. Her flat (in a block of quite recent date) is in truth built on what may be described as 'holy ground', a district called Bonnevoie, which formerly boasted the engine shed of the metre-gauge railway to Hesperange, Mondorf-les-Bains and Remich (replaced in the early 1950s by Chausson buses and similar French-flavoured delights).

Thus one morning — in December 2007, actually — I am surveying the scene from SP's balcony when I am moved to exclaim: "SP! SP! That looked almost as if … as if it was a three-section articulated!"

"What?"

"Yes!" In the next gap. "Look! It is!"

"Yes?"

"Yes!" And in the next gap, "One — two — three!"

This remarkable item had not been present — or at least I had not seen it, which makes me believe the premise to be true, for I must have seen nearly every bus in Luxembourg — on my previous visit a couple of years earlier. SP was kind enough to display some enthusiasm for the machine herself; but then we must bear in mind that, to a psychiatrist, someone who has spent half a century photographing buses (and especially when some maiden is passing in front of them even if obscuring fleet number or registration number) may prove interesting material, and his whims be tolerated and perhaps even studied! Nevertheless SP has generously sent me occasional SMS messages since that day, telling me "Riding on a tripartite now!" (She is a regular passenger on Luxembourg buses, sensible girl!) She considered the term 'three-section articulated' too cumbrous and was pleased to discover her automatic speller could cope with 'tripartite'!

Meanwhile, with observations from the balcony or in the Christmas-lights-clad streets of the city I managed to establish a rough pattern of the beast's schedule. The details are probably of little interest, save only to say one of the terminal points — on route 16 — was Hesperange, near a former light-railway station, and the bus belonged to Voyages Emile Weber, one of several large operators which,

it would appear, share the prime services across the city. Unlike SP I never managed to catch the wretch except with the camera (and that with Decembral difficulty) ... but I made a mental note of its merits and, to these, further inspiration was in due time added.

I must first of all, however, herewith attend to another exploration I undertook at that time. To quote an old Tyneside song, completely inappropriately, 'My Nancy kittled my Fancy ...'

In the declining years of *la belle époque* of French trolleybuses, the late 1960s, I failed to visit Nancy, mainly for the fact that it didn't adopt trolleybuses. Later on, when I had learned the charms of the Saviem Standard SC10, in which, so legend has it, Nancy abounded, I failed again to include it in my travels in search of such, this much to my subsequent regret.

I gathered later that the city became one of those pioneers — Gent in Belgium and Groningen in the Netherlands being others — dedicated to introducing a new generation of trolleybuses. At that moment, though regarding such efforts as praiseworthy, I was proscribed by other commitments (children and preserved buses for example, quite apart from lack of cash!) from inspecting such heroic gestures, and anyway was perhaps quite happy with memories of Vetras and the like in the days of my youth ... Nonetheless,

The joys of Luxembourg! Facing the camera is an MAN artic operated by Demy Cars. To the right is another approach to high carrying-capacity, a tri-axle MAN in the fleet of Voyages Ecker.

In December 2007 Emile Weber's three-part bus steals sedately towards the station in Luxembourg, but with an awful warning on its backside — 'ATTENTION DEPORT IMPORTANT', or 'beware where the rear end may end up'! It is a Van Hool AGG300, 24.8m long.

by some invidious means — notes in *Buses* or tales from my acquaintances — news of Nancy caught my attention.

France, or its principal cities, were by this date (and still are) involved in reintroducing the most flamboyant of tramway schemes. Nancy decided on something different, in fact, if I understand the issue correctly, an upgrade of the trolleybuses to GLT, or Guided Light Transit.

So far as I can gather the origins of this notion were first put into practical form in the generally desolate and unpopulated though summer-tourist-infected Belgian Ardennes in the late 1980s, where a tripartite vehicle was installed to run along what had once been a railway track thenceforth replaced by a central rail (could one say monorail?) to guide it and act as return for current taken from overhead wire via a pantograph, while four suitably disposed axles with normal bus wheels running on concrete laid on either side of the guide rail added the normal — and necessary — support. At a certain point *en route* the machine abandoned the monorail and became a diesel-powered ordinary bus, but, given its monstrous size, it was arguably unsuitable for the curvaceous lanes which marked the several further kilometres of its journey. The scheme disappeared in October 1991, not without one of its vehicles' having meanwhile been exhibited in Bristol — and possibly elsewhere in Britain — where similar plots were being hatched … but, as genealogical tables phrase it, 'without issue'!

Nancy, on the other hand, thought differently. Differently enough, indeed, to turn an adequate trolleybus notion into a GLT. With the turn of the new millennium the main east–west route through the city was opened as a mixture of GLT and common trolleybus instead of diesel, albeit with tripartite vehicles of, it must be admitted, very tram-like appearance. The change from one notion or motion to another was achieved by devices on the road surface — not perhaps entirely unfamiliar to persons who have seen photographs of places where London trams changed from conduit to overhead — and hearsay and evidence on the ground suggest there were several change-points … more than are in use now. Rumour has it that at the opening ceremony one of the cars (or buses?) derailed on a curve, with the mayor on board, and a delay in public operation thus came into force.

Whatever the legend, the truth, so I am well informed, is that while the system operates very adequately as a trolleybus it is restricted in GLT sections to 10km/h on bends or curves and not much higher on straight sections. It is perhaps noteworthy that on picture postcards sold in the shops of Nancy it is proudly described as 'Le Tram',

The charms of the Saviem SC10 eluded the author in Nancy but not elsewhere in France. This example was operating in Caen in 1989.

and the same term applies on exemption plates below no-entry signs, but most up-to-date books in any language on French tramway development tend to ignore its very existence.

On my previous visit to Luxembourg I must have decided either that SP was too busy to drive me to Nancy or that I was too busy in Luxembourg to spend my time on such a foray — or, even more likely, I would arrive in Nancy only to find the business in a state of disarray and non-functional. On this next visit, setting such beliefs at nought, I took a train from Luxembourg; it is an easy enough through journey.

As a student of architecture I wished anyway to see the Michelin-and-elsewhere-Guide-applauded Place Stanilas in Nancy, though in the event it proved rather disfigured by dreadful Christmas decorations including a snowfield and an igloo. Nor is it served

by 'the tram'. As for the latter … the trolleybus section of the route was entirely excellent, the rest was entertaining. To sit in the rear of a tripartite trolleybus and enjoy several right-angle bends — or to watch the switch from trolleybus to GLT — was nearly what transport dreams are made of!

Thus fortified by Nancy, I received more news of other articulations. On these could I write, and how! The introductory sentences are coursing through my head at this moment, but the best-laid schemes of mice and men …

SP and I agreed to visit together diverse destinations where we could indulge in a new generation of articulateds, tripartite or even a return to a lost generation of wheel arrangement newly introduced, along with Baroque architecture and gourmet extravagance. This magnificent scheme fell apart because some of the new generation actually failed to be introduced in the time limit prescribed by the editor and also because SP ran out of holiday-time allotted to her by her translating masters, so we couldn't undertake the excursion anyhow … and thus no essay …

Above: Nancy, December 2007. The vehicle coming from the left is about to engage on the change-pit and become GLT instead of trolleybus, while that coming from the right is already engaged in the latter mode.

Below: Be it GLT or trolleybus, the bends at the terminus of the Nancy service exhibit the ability of a 'tripartite' to cope with the curves.

Six-wheelers

Six-wheel coaches are now more common on Britain's roads than ever before. **Geoff Mills** takes a look.

Left: Arguably the first truly successful three-axle coach in the UK was the twin-steer Bedford VAL of the 1960s. This is an early VAL14, which was new in 1963 to Everall of Wolverhampton. The VAL14 had a Leyland engine, and this example had a 49-seat Plaxton body. It was photographed in 1978 in the ownership of Moss Motor Tours of Sandown, Isle of Wight.

Right: The early 1980s saw an upsurge in interest in three-axle coaches, led by operators wanting high-capacity double-deckers for European holidays. This 1984 Setra S228DT Imperial had been new to Martindale of Ferryhill but by 1994 was in the Red Ensign fleet of Southampton City Transport. It was a 74-seater. As on many double-deck coaches the passenger entrance was ahead of the rear axle.

Left: Plaxton used Neoplan N722/3 underframes for the original version of its Paramount 4000 and between early 1984 and mid-1986 supplied 27 to the National Bus Company, most for use on National Express services. This Ribble vehicle is seen in London's Victoria Coach Station in 1986. It seated 73.

Right: MCW built three-axle Metroliner coaches for NBC and the Scottish Bus Group. In 1985 four were supplied to Wessex National, one being seen in Llandudno in 1990.

Left: In the 1980s Van Hool's integral Astromega found a number of buyers, including Titterington of Penrith, the original owner of this 1984 73-seater. It is pictured at Wembley in 1992 in the ownership of John Pike Coaches of Andover.

Right: Van Hool also offered the 'twin-deck' Astron integral, with lower saloon aft of the rear axle, along with the similar Astral body for mounting on separate chassis. This Astral was based on a tri-axle Volvo B10MT and seated 62 — 50 in the main saloon and 12 on the lower deck. It was new to Harris of Armadale in 1985 but is seen at Knutsford Services on the M6 motorway in 1990 in the ownership of Bruce of Airdrie, operating the company's Londonliner service, which linked Glasgow and surrounding towns with London. The Astral was 4m high.

Left: Another twin-deck body available on the B10MT was Plaxton's 4m-high Paramount 4000RS (the suffix indicating 'rear saloon'). Davies of Pencader operated this 64-seater, configured with 55 seats on the top deck and nine in the lower seating area.

Right: A few B10MT chassis were bodied as single-deck coaches, among them this vehicle delivered to Castleways of Winchcombe in 1985. This view was recorded in 1988, by which time the coach was being operated by Wharfedale of Yeadon. The body was by Finnish builder Ajokki, a rare type to find in UK service.

Left: Neoplan has long been one of the leading suppliers of three-axle double-deck coaches to British operators. Seen at Wembley in 1991 is an N122/3 Skyliner in the fleet of The King's Ferry, Gillingham — hence the GIL registration. It had been new in 1986 (with C-prefix registration) to NAT of Leeds.

Right: Tri-axle single-deckers were still relatively rare in 1990, when this Volvo B10MT entered service with Harry Shaw of Coventry. It had a 49-seat Van Hool Alizee body, built to a height of 3.6m. On most coaches higher than 3.5m a third axle is needed to cope with the extra weight of the bodywork.

Right: The Scania K113TRB with Irizar Century body was a striking coach when it first appeared in the UK in 1993. This example, operated by Dodds of Troon, had been new in 1996 to A&R of Bedfont. It was a 49-seater.

Right: One problem with high-capacity coaches is providing sufficient accommodation for passengers' luggage. Bakers Dolphin of Weston-super-Mare addressed the problem by attaching a trailer to this Volvo B12T, which has a 67-seat Van Hool Astrobel body. It was new in 1997 and is liveried for the company's London Flyer express service.

Left: Neoplan's single-deckers were initially less common in the UK than its double-deckers, but this situation changed in the 1990s. This 1999 Cityliner N116/3 48-seater had been new to Parry's of Cheslyn Hay, which has long been a Neoplan customer. It is seen in 2000 in the ownership of Alec Head of Peterborough, its original T-prefix registration replaced by A11 EAD, arranged to read 'A HEAD'.

Left: In 1999 First Beeline took seven rear-engined Volvo B12Ts with Plaxton Excalibur bodywork for operation on the coach link between Reading and London's Heathrow Airport. By the time of this 2004 photograph they had been demoted to rail-replacement services; now part of the Bristol-based First Coaches fleet, this one is seen outside Ipswich railway station while operating for First Capital.

Left: The Neoplan Skyliner has evolved over the years, and by the late 1990s the styling, whilst still distinctive, seemed a little more restrained than had been the case hitherto. One of a batch of 12 new in 2001 to Trathens of Plymouth, this 65-seater is seen pulling out of Paignton bus station in 2004.

Right: Ayats has had some success in the UK with its three-axle double-deck Bravo, most notably with Translink in Northern Ireland. This stylish Bravo 1 was new in 2001 to Keir of Kemnay, but by 2005 was in the fleet of Ford of Althorne. It was a 75-seater.

Below: In 2007 Mulleys of Ixworth acquired this Van Hool Acron-bodied Volvo B12BT. A 14m-long 59-seater, it had been new the previous year to Focus of Much Hoole.

Right: New in 2008 to Bakers Dolphin of Weston-super-Mare was this 15m-long Scania K470 with Irizar's eye-catching PB body. Despite its extra length the coach has just 40 seats to provide a high standard of comfort on the company's premium Gold Service holidays. It is seen loading in Brixham in 2009.

High hopes, shattered dreams

Stewart J. Brown looks at 10 classic failures — buses which were launched with great fanfare only to vanish before production reached double figures.

IT COSTS A LOT to design a bus. In days of old, men (and possibly women) sat at drawing boards; now they sit at computer screens. But, however they do it, a lot of time and money is spent before the new model takes shape. Then there's the cost of building and testing a prototype — a cost which the manufacturer anticipates will be offset by the sales boom the new model creates.

More often than not, the manufacturer's hopes of success are, to a greater or lesser extent, realised. But sometimes they are not.

It's not always easy to define success and failure. The Leyland National was surely a technical success despite gripes about some aspects of its design — but annual production at the purpose-built Workington factory was only half of what had been planned. Does that make the National a commercial failure?

Then there are the small-scale builders, such as Quest 80 and Ward, who set out with high hopes but soon fall by the wayside. Some might argue that, in an industry dominated by big manufacturers, underfunded start-up businesses have little chance of success, no matter how good their products. So they're not included in this list of high hopes and shattered dreams, which looks only at unsuccessful models from big-name builders. Instead we consider models which failed to reach UK sales in double figures yet were offered by manufacturers which, in the main, sold products by the hundreds, if not the thousands.

That measure — sales in single figures — lets go unremarked some spectacular failures, like the Marshall Minibus, perhaps the most unsuccessful bus of modern times, or the Mercedes-Benz/Wright Urbanranger, which did achieve double-digit sales, albeit only just. Some manufacturers manage to get

things wrong more than once — Iveco/Irisbus for example — with assorted urban bus failures over the years, but for each manufacturer only one failed model is mentioned.

It seems fairer to spread the guilt about a bit.

Mercedes-Benz O.305

Let's start in 1973. That was when one of the most important of the world's automotive manufacturers, Mercedes-Benz, made its first foray into the UK urban-bus market, with the supply to SELNEC PTE of two O.305s. These were bodied by Northern Counties, one of the PTE's two main body suppliers, and were passably attractive dual-door 43-seaters. And, despite the prestige attached to Mercedes' three-pointed star, these buses ran without badges, lest the operation of 'foreign' buses offend the sensibilities of local politicians. When the Mercs joined SELNEC they were its first buses to be sourced from outside the UK.

The O.305s remained unique — if you can use 'unique' to describe two items, which technically you can't, but you get my drift. It would be 20 years before the next full-sized Mercedes-Benz bus (the O.405) entered service in Britain, and not until the arrival of the Citaro in 2000 would Mercedes become a significant supplier to UK bus operators. Mercedes engineered the O.305 in right-hand-drive for other markets, so whatever development costs might have been incurred in producing two chassis for SELNEC were absorbed by vehicles sold elsewhere. On the other hand, one can only hope that when it was selected to build the bodies for the Mercs Northern Counties recognised that there was likely to be little long-term demand for the model and priced its bodywork accordingly.

The enthusiasm for high-capacity single-deckers evinced by some urban operators in the late 1960s began to evaporate when most of the new breed of rear-engined buses proved to be none too reliable, and disappeared completely when the Government legalised the operation of double-deck buses without a conductor. So even if the O.305 had been a wonderful idea, it would have been a wonderful idea at the wrong time.

Foden NC

Coincidentally, perhaps, the next failure involves
Greater Manchester PTE, SELNEC's successor. One
possible interpretation of the Mercedes venture is
that it was the PTE's warning to Leyland, which was
trying to conquer the world — well, at least that part
of the world buying single-deck buses — with the
Leyland National. The National posed a threat to
those independent bodybuilders that had worked
with Leyland on the previous generation of single-
deck chassis for urban bus operation.

By the mid-1970s Leyland's attitude was spreading
to double-deckers, the B15 project — later the Titan

— being promoted as an integral double-decker
to repeat in the double-deck market the success
(questionable as that might be) of the National in
the single-deck market. The B15 sounded alarm bells
in the boardrooms at Metro-Cammell, East Lancs,
Alexander and Northern Counties, all of which
depended on Leyland for the supply of Atlantean,
Fleetline and VRT chassis. It probably also sounded
alarm bells with operators, which were aware that
Leyland's plans would reduce the choice of vehicles
available to them.

There are two ways of looking at Leyland's
attitude. One is that it was being high-handed,

trying to dictate what operators could buy. The other was that it was being rational, trying to produce a high-quality standardised bus, arguing that with just a few specification options virtually any bus could operate anywhere in the UK.

Foden, based in Cheshire — and just outside the PTE's operating area — was a thriving truck manufacturer which had past experience of bus building. And the Foden NC was developed using a Gardner 6LXB engine, easily the most popular power unit among British bus operators, and an Allison gearbox. Consider it a Fleetline for the 1970s.

In the end just seven were built, including one with an East Lancs body, which should thus be considered a Foden EL. Greater Manchester took two, which were delivered in 1976, and in 1977 the

West Yorkshire and West Midlands PTEs joined the party, taking one each. It was South Yorkshire PTE, never one to follow the pack, which specified an East Lancs body for its Foden. The last two were delivered in 1978 to Derby City Transport and to PMT, part of the National Bus Company. The West Yorkshire and PMT buses had low-height bodywork, instantly identifiable by the use of a different style of curved windscreen. As the PMT bus entered service two years after the first Foden NC for Manchester, and no fleet orders had materialised during that time, Foden admitted defeat.

Dennis Falcon V double-deck

Dennis initially designed the Falcon as a single-decker with a Gardner engine, in effect trying to produce a successor to the Bristol RE, which Leyland was desperately trying to kill as it diverted sales from the National. The last 'home market' REs entered service with Halton Borough Transport at the end of 1975 — using the term 'home market' as it was apparently understood by Leyland, which continued 'exporting' REs to Northern Ireland. This was because Ulsterbus dug its corporate heels in and declined to buy the National, aware that if it did so it would be signing the death warrant for Alexander's Belfast factory, which at that time supplied all of its bus bodies.

During this period in its history Dennis was willing to build small numbers of odd buses, and these included a double-deck version of the Falcon V, which used a Mercedes-Benz V6 engine and a Voith automatic gearbox. Nottingham City Transport, always on the look-out for ways to squeeze more seats into a double-decker, had two, with 88-seat dual-door East Lancs bodies. These entered service in 1982, after the first was displayed on the Dennis stand at that year's Motor Show. Both were later sold to Cedar Coaches in Bedfordshire.

In 1984 three were supplied to Greater Manchester PTE, and these had 84-seat Northern Counties bodies. Based initially at Atherton, they later moved to Princess Road and survived to see service with GM Buses South. (It might be fair to point out at this stage that, despite appearing in the first three entries in this list, SELNEC/GMPTE was, in fact, an eminently sensible operator in engineering terms.)

The grand total of Falcon double-deckers was boosted to six by the original East Lancs-bodied demonstrator, which was such an undesirable vehicle that when its period of demonstration ended there were no buyers for it as a bus, and it was sold for conversion to a playbus — an ignominious end for such a youthful vehicle.

Below: A rare view of the Dennis Falcon V demonstrator, operating on hire to Chesterfield Transport in 1983. It had an East Lancs body.
STEWART J. BROWN

Leyland Tiger Cub

Think Leyland Tiger Cub, and the chances are you think of a serviceable lightweight bus/coach chassis of the 1950s. Lightweight was fashionable 50 years ago, and a 45-seat Tiger Cub bus was just 30ft long and weighed around 6 tons — or, if you want to be metric, around 6 tonnes. Anyway, it was light. Just check the weight of a present-day 45-seat bus (admittedly a more sophisticated and user-friendly vehicle) and you'll be astounded at the difference.

But the failed Tiger Cub was a rather different vehicle. In the mid-1980s the British bus industry was in turmoil. Public-sector operators were being privatised, and bus services were being deregulated,

unless you lived in London or Northern Ireland, where different rules applied. There was a growing interest in smaller buses, and Leyland employed two approaches to this turn of events. One was the mid-engined Leyland Swift, which was a success of sorts. The other was the Tiger Cub, which was not.

The Tiger Cub was a mid-sized vehicle built by Leyland's DAB operation in Denmark. The idea was

Above: The second Tiger Cub, delivered to United, was to a different specification, with longer side windows and a deeper windscreen with the destination display behind it. STEPHEN MORRIS

that DAB would build framed vehicles, which would be shipped to Eastern Coach Works at Lowestoft, where they would be trimmed and painted. The Tiger Cub was in fact a high-quality vehicle, far removed from the cheap Transits and Sherpas which would soon be being bought by operators in the real world, and only two were built. One operated for NBC's United Auto (then later for Tees & District); the other was a 43-seat demonstrator. Both ended up in the ownership of Jim Stones of Leigh — a suitably high-quality operation for two buses which could fairly be described as the Rolls-Royces of the midibus market.

MCW Metroliner 400GT

There was a boom in scheduled coach travel in the early 1980s as a result of the deregulation of coaching. This brought new operators — notably the short-lived British Coachways consortium — and saw new marketing and promotional efforts by the main established operators, NBC and Scottish Bus Group. It also brought a search for new high-capacity coaches. Artics were considered and then rejected because they could not use the outside lane on a three-lane motorway, something still legal for conventional coaches back in 1980. Instead NBC turned to double-deckers for its busiest National Express services, and these were supplied by MCW using a modified version of the three-axle Metrobus chassis developed for Hong Kong. Thus was born the Metroliner. This was not an unqualified success —

breakdowns were frequent — but sales were well into double figures, so the original Metroliner doesn't qualify for this list. But the Metroliner 400GT does.

Throughout Europe the standard height for double-deck coaches was 4m. The Metroliner was 4.23m high — which didn't really matter, as none was going to venture into mainland Europe. But MCW clearly had an eye on operators beyond NBC (and SBG), looking at the large number of coach companies buying 4m-high double-deck coaches from Neoplan and Van Hool for trips to the south of France and Spain. Thus was developed the 4m-high 400GT. It was 400cm high. And 'GT' sounded good. Originally 'GT' stood for 'gran turismo' and was used to describe luxurious automobiles used in the 1930s for just that — grand touring in considerable style. By the time of the 400GT the term had been debased by various car manufacturers that had used it to describe small cars with big engines, loud exhausts and go-faster stripes. It would be nice to think that someone at MCW was harking back to its original meaning, in christening the new Metroliner the 400GT.

Be that as it may, it was a flop. With broken-down Metroliners littering the hard shoulders of Britain's motorways, no Continental operator in its right mind was going to buy a 400GT and then send it with two drivers on a non-stop trip to southern Europe. And none did. For its 400GT MCW offered a choice of two engines — the 15.5-litre Gardner 6LYT or the 14-litre Cummins NTE, both rated at 350bhp. (The standard Metroliner was powered by a 290bhp Cummins L10.)

Only three 400GTs were built. The first was a demonstrator, which was exhibited at the NEC bus and coach exhibition in 1986 and was later operated

by West Midlands Travel. Then there was one for
Yorkshire Traction, which entered service in 1988 in
National Express Rapide livery, and another for West
Midlands Travel. Those for WMT were initially used
on the London Liner service. That meant they never
travelled much more than 100 miles from the MCW
factory, which was surely good news for MCW's
service engineers.

Renault PR100

The Renault PR100 was, you might say, the French
Leyland National. It was bought by city-bus
operators throughout France and also found some
export business; interestingly both Nationals and
PR100s were exported to Venezuela.

A stylish bus, launched in 1972 and built
initially by Berliet, the PR100 was a great success.
Until it came to Britain.

In 1988 Renault and Northern Counties
announced they were teaming up and that Northern
Counties would assemble PR100s in Britain: French
flair meets Wigan practicality. The trouble was that
the PR100 design was by this time 16 years old, and
Renault had already launched its successor, the R312.
And the chassis frame looked as though it had been
inspired by the Forth Bridge — yes, the great and
complex railway bridge of 1890, not the slim
(and now over-stressed) road bridge of 1964.

One PR100 was built as a demonstrator in 1988,
and a second was built to London specification and
delivered to the East London fleet in 1989; both
would ultimately gravitate to the fleet of Hornsby
Travel in Lincolnshire. Then came a fleet order:
three for Luton airport. And then came nothing.
Nada. Zilch.

A total of just five PR100s was built at Wigan.

Right: The Iveco TurboCity 100 could fairly be described as a white elephant. It is seen here on demonstration to Solent Blue Line in Southampton. The Alexander R-type body incorporated Iveco's standard TurboCity windscreen. IVECO

The model that superseded the R312 was the Agora, which would later appear in Britain as one of Iveco/Irisbus's many unsuccessful attempts to sell urban buses. But it achieved double-digit sales, so can't be counted here — and, anyway, Iveco had a much more spectacular failure.

Iveco TurboCity 100

The greatest failure of recent times, in terms of sales, has to be the Iveco TurboCity 100 double-decker. Try pronouncing it with the accent on the second syllable so that it scans in the same way as 'atrocity' — tur-bócity. Which seems like a good adjective to coin for this strange bus: it was a tur-bócity.

Anyway, however you choose to pronounce it, the TurboCity was an odd vehicle, based on a 12m-long Italian-style single-deck bus underframe. The concept was shown to various bodybuilders, none of which was too interested, and in the end Iveco got Alexander to body it. The completed bus retained the standard Iveco front dash and windscreen and seated 83, with some compromises in the seating layout to avoid overloading the rear axle. It entered service as a demonstrator in 1991, at which time Iveco had grand plans for both double-deck and single-deck versions of the TurboCity, forecasting sales of an optimistic 480 over five years.

The double-decker remained unique. And even if you throw in the few single-deckers bodied by Alexander (one, in 1992) and Wadham Stringer (half a dozen) you don't reach 48, let alone 480. Indeed, you reach just eight.

Later — in 1998 — Iveco tried a bus version of the EuroRider coach chassis, and that found one PSV buyer, Whitelaw of Stonehouse. It had a Marshall body.

Volvo B7L double-decker

When British operators started switching to low-floor double-deckers in the late 1990s, DAF and Dennis were quick to develop new models. Volvo, on the other hand, decided to do it on the cheap. Its new low-floor double-decker was a right-hand-drive version of its European B7L city bus, and by the time the completed vehicle was unveiled with a striking Northern Counties-built President body at Coach & Bus 97, even Volvo, it would seem, recognised that it had got it wrong.

The B7L had the engine occupying the rear corner of the lower saloon — in a box described as 'the wardrobe in the corner' by one operator that vowed never to buy one. Not, of course, that it was alone in that decision. Because no-one ever did buy a B7L double-decker — other than as an open-top sightseeing bus or with three axles. It also had a long rear overhang. The B7L was shown to various operators — 'demonstrated' would be too strong a word — but never turned a wheel in service. Indeed, it barely turned a wheel at all, and was never registered. It remained unique. Genuinely unique.

This cheapskate approach cost Volvo orders, as customers that might reasonably have been expected to buy the company's new model defected to Dennis. As own-goals go, Volvo's was pretty spectacular. In the end it was back to the drawing board to produce the bus that it should have built in the first place, the undeniably successful B7TL.

TransBus Enviro200

Over the years the lure of orders from London has seduced many manufacturers, and one ill-judged example of this was the TransBus Enviro200 — not the successful bus produced today by Alexander Dennis but an odd vehicle designed with a blinkered eye on London's needs.

The original Enviro200 was possibly the only bus in British history to use different sizes of wheels on the front and rear axles. The front axle had 19½in wheels, the rear 22½in wheels. This allowed the use of single rear wheels with Super Single tyres, which meant a wider gangway over the rear axle.

At this point you might reasonably ask why anyone would particularly want a wider gangway over the rear axle. Well, as it transpired, no-one did, but the TransBus designers had put the exit door on the Enviro200 behind the rear wheels rather than ahead of them. So the wide gangway helped speed up the flow of passengers towards the door. TransBus claimed that the Enviro200 could carry 25% more passengers than a Dart and had a total capacity for 70 — most of whom would stand.

For propulsion the Enviro200 used the Cummins ISBe four-cylinder engine, located in the offside rear corner and driving through a Voith gearbox.

All of this was a very clever answer; but nobody was clear what the question was. London was by the time of the Enviro200 launch — at Coach & Bus 2003 — buying double-deckers in huge numbers, and it was, generally, double-deckers that were replacing ageing Dennis Dart midibuses, something TransBus appears not to have noticed.

The strange wheels and the corner-mounted engine meant that the Enviro200 was compromised when it came to squeezing seats in and therefore was not ideally suited for operators wanting a midibus with just one door — which, of course, covers most of Britain's bus companies.

A red-liveried demonstrator was shown to various supposedly interested parties and was operated briefly in London — and then TransBus collapsed. The bus was then sold to Far East Travel of Ipswich.

MAN Kinetic Plus

You might ask why another manufacturer would want to enter the British double-deck business in 2006, especially after London had completed a massive fleet renewal which entailed an accelerated vehicle-replacement programme to phase out step-entrance double-deckers. But German manufacturer MAN, which builds urban double-deckers for its home market, decided it was time to have a go at the British market and teamed up with East Lancs to launch the Kinetic Plus at EuroBus Expo 2006.

It was certainly a striking bus. East Lancs pulled out all the stops to prove that anyone who still regarded it as a builder of rather homely buses was out of touch. The Kinetic Plus was a head-turner. The chassis was based on MAN's 18.240 but with the 6.9-litre DO8 engine in the rear corner and, most unusually, single rear wheels with extra-wide tyres.

It was also only 4m high, although the plan was that production vehicles would be taller, with more interior headroom. A portal rear axle allowed a full-length low floor.

Unlike some manufacturers (see Iveco above) MAN didn't announce plans to sell hundreds of Kinetic Pluses, instead stating that the prototype would be followed by a second vehicle built to meet the requirements of Transport for London.

If only. In the end the prototype Kinetic Plus remained the only Kinetic Plus, and instead MAN decided to supply engines to Optare (formerly Darwen, and before that East Lancs) for its new integral double-decker, launched as the Rapta at EuroBus Expo 2008 and scheduled to go into production in 2009.

The sole Kinetic Plus was bought by Reading Transport in 2007.

Colourful Manchester

Greater Manchester has over the last 20-odd years been served by a large number of small operators, most of which have now disappeared. **Roy Marshall** illustrates a selection of the region's colourful independents, past and present.

Above: Citibus Tours of Chadderton started local-bus operation in 1983 — three years before deregulation. Initially it ran single-deckers, but later purchases included this ex-Southdown Leyland Atlantean AN68 with Park Royal body. The company was taken over in 1993 by Lynton Travel.

Left: South Manchester Transport ran double-deckers on a route from Piccadilly Gardens, in Manchester city centre, to East Didsbury for a short period in the mid-1990s. Its fleet included this ex-Northampton Bristol VRT with Alexander body.

Right: Bluebird of Middleton started operations in 1988 and is now one of the oldest-established small operators in the Manchester area. It was an early user of low-floor buses, represented by this Dennis Dart SLF with Wright Crusader body, one of four delivered in 1997. Note the BLU registration mark.

Above: Timeline was a buy-out of the bus operations of Shearings in 1992 and retained Shearings' livery. In 1997 it took delivery of nine Optare Excels, one of which is seen leaving Bury Interchange. Timeline's Greater Manchester business was purchased by First Manchester in 1998, by which time it ran almost 50 vehicles.

Right: Glossopdale of Hadfield was among the few buyers of the Marshall Minibus, in 1997 taking four (the biggest fleet of the type outside London), one of which is seen in Ashton-under-Lyne. The business was taken over by Stagecoach in 1999.

Left: Jim Stones of Glazebury runs a small and immaculate fleet on local services in Leigh. Most of the company's vehicles carry apt registrations, such as BUS 51T — 'BUSS IT' — on this 2006 Alexander Dennis Enviro200Dart, the company's first Enviro. The number was previously carried by a Dennis Dart SLF.

Above: JP Travel of Middleton operated this Dennis Dart SLF with comparatively rare UVG bodywork. The FUG registration gives a clue to the vehicle's original owner, Fuggles, of Benenden, Kent. JP Travel still provides bus services in the area.

Left: A Dennis's Dennis. Dennis's of Ashton operated into Manchester city centre with a fleet which included Dennis Tridents with East Lancs bodies. The business was acquired by Stagecoach in 2005.

Above: After starting with second-hand double-deckers in 1986, Wall's of Fallowfield later bought new vehicles, including both double- and single-deck DAFs, for its service from Manchester Piccadilly Gardens to West Didsbury, serving Manchester University on the way. There were four Ikarus-bodied SB220s with N-WAL registrations, delivered in 1995/6. The operation was taken over by Stagecoach in 1996.

Left: An ex-West Midlands MCW Metrobus in the fleet of Stott's of Oldham, which operated in and around the town from 1987 to 1996 and then again from 2003. In recent times the company has concentrated on schools services.

Right: Springfield Coachways operated local services in Wigan from 1992. In 1997 it took delivery of two Optare MetroRiders and three Excels, one of which is seen leaving Wigan bus station. In 1999 the company's services were taken over by First Manchester.

Above: Bullock of Cheadle is an old-established coach operator which diversified into bus operation in 1990, buying both new and used vehicles. Among the new purchases were two Optare Spectras in 1998, which were the first low-floor double-deckers in North West England. Most of Bullock's bus services were taken over by Stagecoach Manchester in 2008.

Below: The old-established Mayne business was for some 50 years the only significant small independent operator running buses in Manchester. The company sold its bus business to Stagecoach in 2008. Two Scanias with 78-seat East Lancs Cityzen bodies were among the older vehicles in the 32-strong fleet at the time of the takeover.

Above: Vale of Manchester operated second-hand coaches and new minibuses, running services from 1990 to 2008, when the business suddenly closed. The coaches included this 12m Leyland Leopard with Duple Dominant IV body, seen outside the Arndale Centre in Manchester in 1996. It had been new to United Counties in 1983.

Left: From 1992 to 2007 ABC — the Atherton Bus Company — ran between Bolton and Leigh using a variety of second-hand vehicles. These included this 1982 Leyland Leopard with ECW body, which had been new (to East Kent) as a coach and therefore offered ABC's customers the benefit of tinted windows, even though it had been re-equipped with bus seats. It is seen leaving Bolton bus station.

Right: Blue Bus of Horwich grew to become a significant operator in the Bolton area. This Volvo Olympian was new in 1999 and had a 77-seat East Lancs Pyoneer body. It was one of five similar vehicles purchased in 1998/9. Blue Bus sold out to Arriva in 2005 but has since restarted in Lancashire, with a small-scale operation in the Preston area.

BRT — the bus of the future?

David Thrower examines Bus Rapid Transit, arguing that it could be the way forward for Britain's bus industry.

OVER THE DECADES there have been a number of significant steps forward in the development of the bus. The first major advance, of course, was the development of the motor bus itself, from the horse bus, in the years immediately prior to World War 1. This was followed by the arrival of the drop-frame chassis, leading by the late 1920s to such classic designs as the Leyland Titan and AEC Regent — buses that would still be familiar, if a little dated, in the late 1950s.

In terms of how buses appeared to the general public rather than to enthusiasts the next really great advance, represented by the Leyland Atlantean and Daimler Fleetline, was the move to front entrances and rear engines, which took bus travel through the 1960s and into the 1970s. However, to the majority of passengers the Metrobuses, Titans and Olympians that followed in the 1980s represented little progress over their predecessors. Nor to the casual observer did a 1990s Dennis Dart look very different from a 1970s Leyland National.

The mould has only finally been broken with the mass conversion of fleets to the low-floor designs of the 21st century. So you could argue that the proverbial great leaps forward were around World War 1, when the traditional motor bus was created, then in the 1950s and '60s, when engines went rearwards or underfloor, and again at the end of the 1990s, when the majority of new buses became fully accessible.

So where to go next? How are bus operators, local authorities and transport professionals going to attract more users to buses? Latest Government traffic forecasts predict a rise in bus use by 2025 of around a third in England, and the remainder of the UK will doubtless seek similar increases.

The BRT concept

One way forward, which is now gaining attention in Britain after a faltering start, is the concept of Bus Rapid Transit, abbreviated to BRT. It takes its name from Light Rapid Transit (LRT), the term applied to modern tramways.

Bus Rapid Transit seeks to bring to bus travel standards similar to those enjoyed by LRT passengers but without the huge expense of laying tracks and (in most cases) erecting overhead electric wires, although the latter are still needed if trolleybuses are involved. It is meant to put distance between the public's downmarket perception of bus travel of the past and a brave new future. It's certainly not just a case of new eye-catching styling and liveries being applied to traditional buses.

The main features of BRT as now increasingly being practised worldwide are that it uses reserved routes or bus-only lanes or streets wherever possible, so that the bus in effect runs on a reserved track for much or even most of the way. Bus Rapid Transit also has high-quality roadside facilities, more akin to tram stations than bus stops.

The buses themselves can be articulated — or even double-articulated — and can be diesel, diesel-electric or powered by other forms of propulsion. They can also be conventional steered vehicles or guided buses, the latter with the driver steering the vehicles across road junctions and when passing other buses but with small guide-wheels or other guidance systems being used on the trunk sections wherever circumstances allow it. This is designed to give a smoother ride and to enable the bus to run accurately through restricted clearances such as under bridges.

For what is often seen as a novel concept BRT has a surprisingly long history. Worldwide, the pioneering guided systems are regarded by many as being the busways in Essen, Germany, and Adelaide, Australia. Another well-known system that gained early attention, this time involving buses running on reserved roads without guidance, was that in Curitiba, Brazil.

But the UK can still proudly lay claim to one of the pioneering systems, at Runcorn, built at the end of the 1960s and opened in 1972. The Runcorn Busway, as it has always been known, pre-dates the term 'Bus Rapid Transit' but at least encompasses the reserved-track element. It was designed as a figure of

An early attempt to create a new image for bus services was the Stevenage SuperBus, launched by London Country in 1971. This 1974 view features, from left to right, a Leyland National, a Metro-Scania and an AEC Swift in the distinctive SuperBus livery.
STEWART J. BROWN

eight, and although one loop has since closed, due to the loss of industry from the area, the other, serving what used to be known as Shopping City, plus some spur sections, remains very much as originally conceived.

Surprisingly, despite subsequent developments overseas with BRT, there was little progress elsewhere in the UK following the initial trail-blazing development at Runcorn. Introduced in 1971, the SuperBus network in Stevenage offered an above-average bus product but relied on ordinary roads and ordinary stops. Although bus lanes and bus-only streets gained favour, and there were attempts — embodied in the Suburban Express and Business Commuter variants of the Leyland National — at improving the ambience of bus travel, there seemed to be no concerted effort to re-package bus travel as something significantly better.

In 1986 came bus deregulation, and in many ways this made developing BRT much more difficult, as operators competed for what was all too often the bottom end of the market, many using junk buses such as DMS Fleetlines that should by that time have been *en route* to the scrapyard.

Overseas developments

Meanwhile BRT was slowly gaining a foothold elsewhere in the world, as metropolitan authorities struggled to find the funds to pay for light rail systems. Thus, although there has been a flurry of interest recently in the UK, the real progress has been made overseas, using diesel buses or trolleybuses, mainly unguided and running on bus lanes.

France, in particular, has been at the forefront of developments with trolleybuses. Caen has installed a guided-trolleybus system, using a central guide rail. Nancy too has used a guide rail, but there have been some problems, and future extensions of BRT may rely on optical guidance. Clermont-Ferrand operates the Translohr system, which looks (and, unfortunately, costs) much the same as a full tramway but actually employs multi-articulated trolleybuses guided by central rail. On such systems the stops are like full LRT-type stations, and passengers have the impression of riding on an LRT system instead of a high-spec trolleybus. In Spain, meanwhile, Castellon de la Plana, in Valencia, has an even more interesting trolleybus BRT route that uses optical guidance based on twin dotted lines on the road, which are followed by an on-board camera.

What all these bus-based and trolleybus-based systems have in common is that the authorities and operators have set out to create something that is tangibly and visibly much better than just plain-vanilla bus travel. Many members of the travelling public, both in Britain and overseas, have an antipathy towards buses. They will get out of their cars to travel by BRT, with some exhortation (backed by high car-parking charges), but not by any ordinary bus.

New UK schemes

The British bus industry is sometimes accused of conservatism and a 'we've always done it like that' attitude, and perhaps this goes some way towards explaining why BRT until recently made very slow progress in the UK. However, a sudden flurry of activity now seems set to make up for lost time.

Crawley's Fastway system, including 1.5km of guided busway and a further 5.8km of unguided bus lanes, was launched in 2003. Patronage on the affected routes immediately rose sharply and has continued to increase. Still in the South East, Fastrack, serving the Dartford, Greenhithe and Gravesend areas, was implemented in 2006/7. This system includes segregated lanes and traffic signal priorities, together with high-technology information and ticketing.

A much higher-profile scheme, which has caused great controversy among rail supporters, has been the conversion to guided busway, at a total cost of about £120 million, of the Cambridge-St Ives route, which at 25km will be the longest such system in the world. A further part-guided, part-public-road scheme, is the busway linking Luton Airport to Luton, Dunstable and Houghton Regis, costing about £85 million. The high cost of these schemes has caused some sharp intakes of breath, and one must hope that each proves to be an outstanding success.

A far cheaper (if lower-tech) version of BRT was introduced in York by FirstGroup with its 'ftr' (text-messaging speak for 'future') articulated Volvo/Wright 'StreetCars', which, perhaps more than anything else, have put BRT on the map in the UK. These cannot be confused with ordinary single-deck buses, and they make London's Mercedes-Benz Citaros look positively staid. Wrightbus is to be congratulated for one of the most radical styling jobs ever carried out on a British bus.

Meanwhile, other, much smaller trial schemes have got underway elsewhere in the UK. Leeds has introduced a mixture of guided and unguided busways on the Scott Hall Road routes. It isn't full BRT, but it's a start. Bradford too has a section of guided busway on the Manchester Road routes, while StrretCars have been introduced in Leeds and Swansea.

Amongst planners there now appears to be a steadily emerging consensus that BRT can help solve urban congestion problems at an affordable price.

The essential features of a scheme are recognised as being substantial seating capacity — rather than 'cattle-truck' standee vehicles — and low emissions, with good-quality roadside facilities, off-bus ticket sales, real-time information and a smart and futuristic image.

The future

BRT is still seen by many critics as LRT's poor relation, a sort of cheap substitute, and is sometimes strongly opposed as being inferior by the proponents of light rail and even suburban rail schemes. This is a pity. It is far more positive to see it as a sort of 'super-bus' system, a step up from ordinary buses, rather than a step down from trams.

To the planners of transport systems BRT has four future key advantages. Firstly, it can be built affordably, perhaps using existing roads and bus lanes in the first instance before the installation of genuine busways at a later date, as and when traffic builds up. And it offers a good-quality system that can be marketed as an alternative to the private car.

Secondly, it offers open access to a range of bus operators. In deregulated Britain this is a major advantage, as a number of different bus operators can make use of any new system, subject to agreeing to provide buses of sufficiently high quality. This could result in any BRT infrastructure being used to the maximum, by a network of routes serving a wide range of destinations.

The third and most important advantage, however, is that BRT avoids sizeable up-front expenditure on 'big-ticket' items required by the likes of light rail but which in themselves do not actually do very much for passengers' travel experience — underground service diversions, track-laying, substations, poles, wires and depots. Substations, poles and wires will, of course, be needed for a trolleybus BRT network, but as most BRT is diesel-powered most of this heavy initial expense can be side-stepped.

Finally, BRT networks can be altered, re-planned, extended or diverted much more easily than rail-based schemes.

For the urban-transport planners of the 21st century, in Britain and elsewhere, BRT looks like an idea whose time has finally come. It won't suit every town and city, and there will be plenty of places where it is unaffordable, leaving buses to continue running on ordinary streets, or where light rail or the reopening of a full suburban railway line is still the best option. But it offers a very useful halfway-house between the bus and the tram or train, and one which many would regard as long overdue.

Right: Not quite BRT, but the guided busway in Leeds affords an exclusive right of way for operators providing appropriate vehicles. This is the opening event, which explains why the Arriva bus is facing in the wrong direction. Both the Arriva and the First bus are Volvo B7TLs with Alexander ALX400 bodywork.
ANDREW JAROSZ

Left: The use of guide-wheels on buses ensures accurate positioning at bus stops, facilitating access for passengers in wheelchairs or pushing baby buggies — something not always possible at stops where inconsiderate parking can prevent the bus from getting to the kerb. This First bus is a 1998 Scania L113 with 40-seat Wright body.
ANDREW JAROSZ

Right: The Thames Gateway Fastrack service is operated by Arriva with a fleet of high-specification Wright-bodied Volvo B7RLEs.
GAVIN BOOTH

Left: A flavour of the quality of BRT is given by the Wrightbus Streetcars operated by First in Leeds and York. The vehicles create a first-class image, but in both cities they operate without the benefit of expensive infrastructure, relying instead on bus lanes and bus priorities.
STEWART J. BROWN

Left: The city of Merida, Venezuela, has dual-mode trolleybuses which are fitted with diesel engines and operate on a reserved busway with proper stations which have high-level platforms. Although Venezuela drives on the right the Trolmerida buses drive on the left, which allows the use of island platforms located centrally on the busway. The vehicles are based on Mercedes-Benz O405GN chassis with Bombardier electrics and Hispano bodies.
STEWART J. BROWN

Left: Las Vegas has high-quality bus services and is expanding them with a fleet of 50 Wright StreetCar hybrids for use on the city's ACE Rapid Transit operation. The StreetCars follow the delivery in 2004 of 10 Irisbus Civis BRT-style vehicles which feature optical guidance.
WRIGHTBUS

Right: There are more than 100 Irisbus Cristalis trolleybuses in operation in Lyon, in both 12m rigid and 18m articulated form. Leeds is considering vehicles like this for what it calls its New Generation Transport system. STEWART J. BROWN

Below: New Flyer has supplied six hybrids to Lane Transit District in Eugene, Oregon, for its EmX BRT service. These have doors on both sides — making them even more like trams — and cost almost $1 million each. The service started in 2007. LANE TRANSIT DISTRICT

Right: BRT is appearing in countries around the world. This busway is in Istanbul, Turkey, and is served by four-axle 20m-long Mercedes-Benz CapaCity artics, of which operator IETT has 250 in service or on order. Like the Trolmerida operation in Venezuela, Istanbul's busway has vehicles driving on the left and serving centrally-located platforms. DAIMLER AG

Leeds' leading independent

Andrew Jarosz charts the story of Black Prince, one of the longest-established independent operators to serve the city of Leeds.

All photographs by the author

Everyone has his/her own favourite independent bus operator. After all, independents represent a dying breed — but during their lifetime the routes, the vehicles and the characters that made up the companies created interest and made a lasting impression on individuals, in an increasingly corporate world in which the big groups are standardising operations. Statistics are hard to come by, but the remaining independent bus operators which started up operations in the early part of the 20th century can probably be counted on the fingers of both hands. In 1986 bus-service deregulation spawned a host of new independent bus operators, eager to cash in on Transport Minister Nicholas Ridley's vision of a growing bus market which was to be stimulated by unfettered competition. Some were new start-up bus operators, many were coach operators that had already developed a taste for bus operation with contract and school work, and others were established bus operators that fancied expanding their route networks. In addition, a lot more operators were waiting in the wings to see how the concept of deregulation was going to pan out in practice.

Looking back, it's hard to think of any companies that started up in October 1986 that are still around today. There are independents that started up after 1986, but most of the companies founded in the 1980s have either faded away or been gobbled up by one of the larger groups. But the one which will be remembered with affection for years to come is Black Prince of Morley, which lasted 36 years and operated local bus services from the very first day of deregulation.

Black Prince was not just a true family business but was personified by its founder, Brian Crowther, who in later years was ably supported by his son David, who hadn't been born when the company was founded in 1969. Brian purchased his first coach — a Bristol LS6G — in 1968, but the new company was formed a little later when he teamed up with long-term friend Bert Colley. The company name was suggested by a statue in the middle of City Square in Leeds, although the prince has absolutely no historical connection with the city!

By the late 1970s the fleet size included around half a dozen coaches, and the company had dabbled with double-deckers, although the majority of its work was in the contract and private-hire market. An important landmark was the assumption of the Wakefield–Blackpool express service on behalf of National Express, which was to lead to the takeover of the service and its subsequent commercial operation until coaching was abandoned in 1997.

When deregulation came Black Prince registered four routes, amongst them the X54, a commercial service between Morley and Leeds, and a local Morley 'Shophopper' based on the company's experience of providing a contract service for Morley Market Traders during the 1984 West Riding bus strike. These two routes remained the backbone of the company's operations, although additional commercial and tendered routes added over the years built a comprehensive competitive network in Leeds.

As any fledgling operator would have done in those days, Black Prince did not seek confrontation with the incumbent operator but was looking to fill gaps created by the drastic scaling back of services by Yorkshire Rider. Rider, on the other hand, was keen to stop the newcomer in its tracks and laid on extra buses to swamp the Morley route. Black Prince responded by introducing a new stopping service, 54, which went through the city and ended up at Moor Grange, the X54 being renumbered X51 and reduced to a peak-hour and evening service. Rider then put on Freight Rover minibuses, at least 12 per hour, and battle was joined, with all the usual tactics of stand blocking, extras, additional duplication, staff poaching and so on. Nevertheless, Black Prince survived the onslaught, and the Yorkshire Rider minibuses eventually departed, but competition on the Morley corridor continued. Another route —

the 53, from Morley's Glen Estate to Sainsbury's at Moortown — was added, giving at least 12 buses per hour between Morley Town Hall and Leeds via Churwell Hill and at least six per hour using Wide Lane, these totals including journeys worked by Arriva, which had taken over the Taylors service.

In the early years enough tendered work — taking services as far as Huddersfield — was won to justify the opening of a main depot at Gildersome. But with cutbacks by Metro (West Yorkshire PTE) much of this either disappeared or was won or registered commercially by Arriva, successor to the West Riding group. Subsequently more central premises with more workshops were purchased at Fountain Street, in the centre of Morley, although Brian's original base adjacent to his home in Texas Street, remained

in use, particularly for preserved vehicles.

The post-deregulation development of Black Prince can be conveniently divided into two distinct parts, the first being an era of growth which saw the active fleet peak in 1995 at more than 60 vehicles. During this period the company was constantly upgrading its fleet from a motley collection of second-hand Atlanteans, Metropolitans, Metrobuses, Routemasters, Leopards and Nationals until it majored in on the Ailsa B55 double-decker, eventually owning nearly 40, which made it by then the largest fleet of its type in the country. The Ailsas were sourced from all over the country and included all three supplied new to London Transport, most notably the infamous V3, which was unique in having two staircases and, as delivered, the exit door

Left: **Seen in Leeds city centre with a Yorkshire Rider minibus behind it is a Black Prince Bristol RE which had been new in 1974 to City of Oxford. Although it has a bus-style ECW body it was fitted out from new as a semi-coach with 49 high-backed seats. Note the 'Best Bus for You' wording below the windscreen and the Leyland badge on the grille; the bus had a Leyland engine.**

Right: **Leyland Nationals were acquired from a variety of sources. This 11.3m model had been new in 1978 to South Wales Transport.**

Left: A small number of Routemasters was operated. This immaculate example in Leeds' City Square carries its London Transport fleet number, RM2060, in the correct position on the cab side.

Right: More typical of the fleet in the mid-1990s is this Park Royal-bodied Leyland Atlantean. It had been new in 1972 to SELNEC PTE.

Left: Ailsas featured prominently in Black Prince's operations. This Alexander-bodied bus had been new to Central SMT. It is loading in central Leeds for a trip back to Morley, where Black Prince was based.

aft of the rear axle. Predictably LT's unions had objected to this arrangement, and the rear door was panelled over, but this was the least of V3's problems, for when the bus reached Morley in 1992 it was as a source of spares, having overturned in an accident and been severely damaged. Brian and David, who by now had taken over the engineering side of the business, decided that a full rebuild was possible, and the bus became a long-term 'spare-time' project, eventually entering service 12 years later, in 2004 — long after all other Ailsas had departed!

In 1994 three routes were acquired from Amberley Travel of Pudsey, when that operator folded, and the 88 service from Thornbury through Leeds to Crossgates was extended at either end to Bradford in the west and Colton in the east. The retention of the blue livery used by Amberley represented the start of route-branding by Black Prince, and the subsequent shade of darker blue was pretty close to the original colours of Samuel Ledgard, whose buses at one time were the only link between Leeds, Pudsey and Bradford.

Something of a watershed year, 1995 saw the arrival of the first new buses purchased by the company — four MAN/Optare Vectas — and its last new coach, an EOS 90. The nature of the work undertaken was also changing; until this point it had comprised the traditional mix of contracts, schools, commercial and tendered bus services and coaching, but by now the company was focusing increasingly on bus services, as the network in Leeds continued to expand. To some extent this was dictated by a Traffic

Left: **Black Prince acquired all three of the Alexander-bodied Ailsas which had been purchased by London Buses as part of a vehicle-evaluation programme in the mid-1980s. They retained their London fleet numbers, as demonstrated by V2 in Leeds.**

Right: **The high standard of presentation for which Black Prince became noted is apparent on this impressive Leyland Atlantean. It is an unusual 33ft-long AN68C/2, with 83-seat Northern Counties body, and had been new to another Yorkshire independent, Longstaff of Mirfield.**

Commissioner's hearing in 1996 which resulted in Black Prince's vehicle authorisation being reduced to 36, and the last of the contract and school journeys, which were only marginally profitable, was given up. Coaching was wound up soon afterwards, and thereafter the operation concentrated almost entirely on urban commercial routes, plus a few tendered services.

Not content with an operational fleet of 36, David now applied for 12 discs in his own name, and thus was born Leeds Suburban Buses, operating a new route — 100, branded as the 'Silverline Link' — from Bramley and the University to Clarence Dock (where new student housing was built). This metamorphosed into service 752 to Kirkstall, and LSB started trading as Leeds City Transport, reviving the livery worn by the one-man-operated buses of the erstwhile municipal fleet and showing how modern-day Scania 'deckers would have looked had not LCT been absorbed by West Yorkshire PTE in 1974. To the casual observer the livery was a perfect copy, but closer scrutiny showed that the city coat of arms (within the fleetname) had been modified so as not to offend the city fathers. In reality all but the stuffiest jobsworths at the council were proud to see the city's identity being smartly displayed on very modern buses. Also used occasionally in service was a (genuine) former Leeds City Transport Roe-bodied Leyland PD3, one of a number of preserved half-cab buses which kept Brian in touch with his enthusiast side.

Another initiative at the end of the 1990s was a determined attack on the student market with the setting up of route 63B from Clarence Dock to Bodington Hall, just outside the ring road to the north of the city. The route passed the two universities and through Headingley on the notorious Otley Road (Leeds' equivalent of Manchester's Wilmslow Road), where at peak times 'wall to wall' buses competed with abominable traffic congestion. Brian's solution was to buy two Routemasters to add to a preserved example, known affectionately as 'Rudolf', that was already in stock, offer a special 50p student fare and try to outrun First with more-manœuvrable vehicles that were crew-operated. Ultimately, however, the figures did not add up, First having sewn up the pre-payment market, and the route was eventually withdrawn.

Apart from route-branded buses and those in overall advertising liveries (of which there were many) every one of Black Prince's vehicles had its own distinct livery using a blend of the three main colours of red, maroon and yellow. The fleet livery changed from green to red in the late 1980s, but perhaps only the enthusiasts realised that every time a bus was repainted, the blend and proportions of the colours changed. Buses were painted all-over red when the company was challenged by Taylors, which operated red Ailsas, and one double-decker was painted with wheels between decks giving the impression of two single-deckers perched on top of each other.

The fleet also improved. One by one the Ailsas departed, to be replaced by Marshall-bodied Scania double-deckers that had originated with Newport, along with a few Olympians, plus a pair of Northern Counties-bodied Scanias new to Greater Manchester — one of which retained its latter-day Stagecoach livery long enough to panic FirstGroup management into believing that its great rival had finally gained a foothold in West Yorkshire! Gradually the Scania, with bodywork by Alexander or East Lancs, became the chosen workhorse, sources including MTL North, Nottingham City Transport, Kentish Bus and Travel West Midlands, whence came a final five (in 2003) which entered service after extensive upgrading. Sadly the company's intention in 2002 to order two brand-new Scania/East Lancs OmniDekkas, which would have been its first low-floor buses, never came to fruition.

The single-deck fleet had always been small, but one notable and long-serving member was an Alexander-bodied Scania that had been supplied to London Buses in 1989 and was acquired by Black Prince less than two years later. Over time the subject of two extensive rebuilds, which amongst other things saw its original Scania gearbox replaced by Voith transmission, it was reputed to be the fastest bus in the fleet and was often used on the tightly timed Morley locals. However, despite a brief flirtation with Wadham Stringer-bodied Scania single-deckers from Newport, Black Prince preferred to buy new or nearly new single-deckers. In 1996 local builder Optare supplied the first of four 49-seater Prismas based on the Mercedes-Benz O405 chassis, and over the next five years a further four identical buses were acquired second-hand, having initially seen service with Tillingbourne of Cranleigh or Henderson of Hamilton. In 1997/8, meanwhile, came four East Lancs-bodied Scania L113s — three supplied new and one acquired, when only a year old, from Bigfoot Buses of nearby Armley — while in 1998/9 two Optare MetroRiders were bought new for contract work.

Brian said that his Mercedes-Benz buses were the best ever built and claimed that the reliability of the Scania 'deckers, which did cost a little more to run, was hard to beat. Nevertheless, there were clouds

Right: Among the more unusual buses owned by Black Prince was this pre-production Leyland Olympian, which was supplied to Greater Manchester PTE in 1980. It had a Northern Counties body. It was sold for preservation and has since been restored to original condition.

Left: In later years second-hand Scanias featured prominently in the fleet. This 1982 Marshall-bodied BR112, in Leeds Suburban livery, was one of 20 acquired from Newport Transport.

Right: An older Scania/Marshall, also acquired from Newport, in the blue livery which was reminiscent of that used by Samuel Ledgard, a Leeds independent which sold out to the West Yorkshire Road Car Co in 1967.

Left: It might look like an Alexander R type, but this is an East Lancs copy of the Scottish builder's design, on an ex-Newport Scania N112. It is seen in Leeds City Transport livery, of the style used by the municipal fleet in the late 1960s and early 1970s.

Left: This former London Buses Scania N113 — registered by Scania with an appropriate '113' number — was less than two years old when it headed north to join the Black Prince fleet. It had a 51-seat Alexander PS-type body.

Left: Among the Optare Prismas owned were three 1997 examples which were acquired from Tillingbourne in 2001. The Prisma was based on the Mercedes-Benz O405 chassis.

on the horizon, notably in the form of escalating insurance premiums; these were costing the company more than £1,200 per day, and Brian feared that, as the number of trivial (not to mention fraudulent) claims increased, they would continue to rise. Moreover, after 35 years of running the family business and 18 of head-to-head competition on bus routes in Leeds, Brian, now 64, was suffering health problems. It thus came as no surprise when, in February 2005, he announced that he was preparing to retire from the transport industry, having reached agreement for the transfer of his business to First West Yorkshire.

Before it could be completed the deal, which would give First a near-monopoly of bus services in Leeds, had to be cleared by the Office of Fair Trading, and as part of the investigation it was revealed that Black Prince had made no profit for more than two years, Brian admitting that he had been actively seeking a purchaser for the business for a number of years and had made approaches to nearly 60 parties.

At the time Brian said that he had no plans for the future, but it was to take him months to wind up all the affairs. "The whole thing fills me with sadness," he said, "but the reality is that costs are going up, and we are all getting older." He blamed insurance costs, fuel costs, First's day tickets and Metro's parsimonious attitude to secured services

and ticketing revenue for making the margins tighter. "It's not an easy industry today, but I've enjoyed every day, and I have some of the friendliest drivers you will ever meet. Some of them have remained with me from day one, all those years ago!"

First did not take over the business, which in 2004 had a turnover of £2.8 million, but paid for the right to take over the eight commercial routes and some tendered workings plus up to 100 staff, including more than 70 drivers. Brian disposed of his premises, vehicles and equipment through various means, First ultimately acquiring 16 Alexander-bodied Scania double-deckers and the sole remaining East Lancs-bodied single-decker after operations ceased on 31 July 2005. As late as 2009 three of the double-deckers and the single-decker remained in service in Leeds, although all the acquired services have been recast beyond recognition.

Regrettably, the postscript is a sad one. Brian did not live long to enjoy his retirement, passing away early in 2008 after a short period of illness. Industry colleagues and former employees speak affectionately of the man who for so many years led the business from the front. In the end, competition on the road wore him down, but he enjoyed running buses to the point where he retained unprofitable workings because he believed in providing a comprehensive service to his passengers.

Right: Among the Black Prince vehicles which passed to First was this Alexander-bodied Scania N113 which had been acquired from Travel West Midlands in 2003. New in 1990, it would remain in service in Leeds until the spring of 2009.

My municipal neighbours

David Wayman spent the 1960s working in Scotland. Here he describes the three municipal fleets run by his near-neighbours when he was based first in the South West and then in the North East.

D URING THE PERIOD 1960-9 I lived and worked in Scotland and always had good neighbours, not just human ones but neighbouring municipalities that owned and operated their own public-transport services. Three of these were, in turn, Glasgow, Dundee and Aberdeen. Much interest and variety there, what?

Glasgow, population then some one million, was the first and furthest from my then base in Stranraer — a spectacular four-hour journey by Western SMT double-deck bus, taking in the magnificent Firth of Clyde, with its dramatic vistas of islands, peninsulas and mountains. And, of course, Glasgow was a public-transport enthusiasts' delight, for as well as motor buses and trolleybuses the city still had trams. Oh, wonderful! But by 1960 fewer than 800 were left from the 1950 total of nearly 1,200, and they were to disappear altogether in 1962.

The Corporation buses, trolleybuses and trams ran to or through places with colourful and, indeed, poetic names like Sandyhills, Broomielaw, Kelvindale, Cowcaddens, Castlemilk, Crossmyloof, Crossstobs (yes, three 'esses' together), Penilee, Carmunnock, Possil, Nitshill, Pollokshaws and, perhaps most colourful of all, the magnificent Auchenshuggle. This was at the eastern end of tram service 9 from Dalmuir West, which ran through Clydebank, Scotstoun, then along Argyle Street and London Road, the A74, to reach Auchenshuggle.

Scores of older tramcars were of a basic design dating back to the turn of the century, albeit with more recent electrical and mechanical equipment. These were the magnificent four-wheel single-truck 'Standards', surely the archetypal traditional British tramcar. Some late-1930s cars known as 'Kilmarnock Bogies' were of generally similar appearance. Other bogie cars of the late '30s, the 'Coronations', had streamlined features typical of the period. There were also some broadly similar early-postwar specimens, the 'Cunarders', plus a further half-dozen built in 1954, the 'New Coronations'.

Besides the trams Glasgow had 190 trolleybuses, double- and single-deck, of BUT, Leyland, Daimler and Sunbeam manufacture. Class TB consisted of 124 BUT two- or three-axle double-deckers with Metro-Cammell or Crossley bodywork, while the

Left: Glasgow's trolleybus fleet included 20 Sunbeams, five of which had Alexander bodywork — the first trolleybuses to be bodied by Alexander.
STEWART J. BROWN

TBS type comprised 21 single-deck BUTs with two axles, the last 10 of particular interest in being built to a special 34ft 6in length with 50-seat Burlingham bodies, seemingly enormous. The others were of normal length with 36-seat bodywork by Weymann or East Lancs. There were also 30 three-axle Daimlers (TD class) and 20 two-axle Sunbeams (TG, indicating Guy).

Clearly, for tram and trolley buffs Glasgow was very much the place to be. But in 1960 the city was also home to some 900 motor buses (all but about 70 of them double-deckers, the majority with front engine and rear entrance), a number growing as the tram fleet shrank. Motor buses wore a livery of apple green upper half and yellow lower, separated by a cream band. This was in the course of replacing an earlier combination of orange and green, with cream window surrounds and roof. Motor buses were

classified and numbered according to chassis make. Of Glasgow's unrebodied postwar double-deckers AECs were given an 'A' class prefix, Daimlers 'D' and Leylands 'L', the solitary Crossley being numbered C1. Single-deckers had an 'S' suffix, and older chassis which had been rebodied were generally suffixed 'R'.

The 429 AEC Regents comprised an assortment. The majority — 265 — were Mk IIIs dating from the period 1948-51, with bodywork by Metro-Cammell, Crossley, Northern Coachbuilders or Weymann, all seating 56. A further 75 were 1955 Mk Vs with identical Alexander or Weymann bodywork, both types 60-seaters, while the newest were 89 30ft-long 1960 Mk Vs with 72-seat forward-entrance Alexander bodies; all of the Regent Vs sported a new-look front with vertical slats for the grille, instead of the traditional bonnet and exposed radiator shell of the Regent IIIs or the smart Rover-like grille

Left: AEC did well in Glasgow's early postwar orders, between 1948 and 1951 supplying 265 Regent IIIs. Most had this style of body, built by both Metro-Cammell and Weymann. HARRY HAY

Right: Bodywork by Alexander and Weymann to this design was supplied to Glasgow on Leyland Titan, Daimler CVG6 and, as seen here, AEC Regent V chassis. Glasgow specified a non-standard grille on its Regent Vs. HARRY HAY

normally fitted to Regent Vs. The Mk IIIs and 27ft-long Mk Vs had the AEC preselector gearbox, but the 30ft-long Mk Vs featured the semi-automatic unit, with two-pedal control. Moreover, instead of the usual AEC 9.6-litre engine the 75 Mk Vs of 1955 had the alternative 8.4-litre Gardner 6LW and so sounded rather like Daimler CVG6s. The Weymann bodywork on the 1951 Mk IIIs was interesting. At that time Metropolitan-Cammell-Weymann was a marketing and patent-holding organisation for the Metropolitan-Cammell Carriage & Wagon Co of Birmingham and Weymann of Addlestone. Before the lightweight era of the mid-1950s each tended to produce bodies to its own distinctive design, but those 100 Weymann-built bodies of 1951 for Glasgow most unusually were of Metro-Cammell design, with features that could be seen to be derived ultimately from Met-Cam's 1930s products.

Turning to the D-class double-deck Daimlers of 1949-51: there were a score of 8.6-litre CVD6/Northern Coachbuilders, 39 CVD6/Alexander, one rare 10.6-litre CD650/Alexander, five CVD6/Scottish Aviation and one CVD6/Mann Egerton. Another solitary specimen was a CVG6/Alexander of 1954, introducing to Glasgow the Daimler tin front radiator cowl and bonnet then fashionable. Daimlers delivered up to 1951 sat 56 passengers. Others, new 1955-9, comprised 49 8.4-litre CVG6/Weymann 60-seaters and 100 CVG6/Alexander with 61 seats. One, D217, distinctively registered FYS 999, was a solitary CVD650-30/Alexander 73-seater of 30ft length, sporting a Manchester-style front cowl. It was followed by 45 CVG6s and five CVD6s, all 27ft-long 61-seaters, also with Manchester-style grilles. While Daimler engines were most refined, Gardners were considerably more economical in terms of both fuel consumption and maintenance costs. The highest-numbered Daimler, D268, was not to arrive until 1963, being Glasgow's solitary Fleetline, with Alexander bodywork, by then Glasgow's standard. But perhaps the most interesting were 43 DS-class CVD6 chassis new in 1948, on which Glasgow Corporation — well experienced in the construction of sound tramcar bodies at its Coplawhill Car Works — had built the dual-door single-deck bus bodies.

Of Glasgow's L-class Leylands the first 23 — regrettably not showing their faces much when I was around — were 1935 Titan TD4s with that lovely-sounding and so-smooth 8.6-litre engine and humming, crooning constant-mesh gearbox. They had postwar Alexander bodies. Unlike neighbouring big-company operators Glasgow Corporation eschewed the early postwar Leyland Titan PD1, with its somewhat harsh-sounding 7.4-litre engine, but did favour the succeeding 9.8-litre Titan PD2. Examples acquired during 1955-60 comprised 25 of type PD2/25 (7ft 6in wide), followed by 300 of type PD2/24 (8ft wide). In 1960/1 along came 140 30ft-long PD3/2s. These PD2s and PD3s sported the then-fashionable Leyland tin front — rather like a voluminous party skirt — except for L398, which had the revised St Helens arrangement made from glass-reinforced plastic. There were also 30 dual-door Leyland Worldmaster single-deckers, the LS class.

Alexander built the bodywork on all Leylands save for 75 PD2s and 25 PD3s that, most interestingly, had bodies built by GCT Car Works to Alexander design. The bodies on the TD4s and PD2s were rear-entrance, seating 52 on the TD4s and 60 or 61 on the PD2s, whereas the PD3s had 72-seat forward-entrance bodywork. The PD2 and PD3 chassis featured Leyland's Pneumocyclic gearbox, with semi-automatic actuation and two-pedal control; this was a relatively new concept at the time and was by no means embraced enthusiastically by operators of front-engined buses, particularly those outside the

municipal sector. But a Pneumocyclic just had to be sampled. A quick peep over the driver's left shoulder and into the cab revealed on the left — where the gear-stick usually was — a floor-mounted pedestal with small projecting lever, which he moved as normally for ratio changes. At stops he let it idle through the fluid transmission in starting ratio — always second except for uphill starts. There then followed a gentle take-off followed by a smooth progression up to fourth, with little noise from the transmission.

Albion buses were relatively rare in municipal service, but of course their builder was a Glasgow concern, and understandably the Corporation operated a proportion pre- and postwar. The letter 'A' having already been taken, the postwar Albion

Venturers were given a 'B' prefix and comprised 24 of type CX19 with Roberts bodywork, a further 24 CX19/Metro-Cammell, 40 CX37/Roberts, 10 CX37/Croft, 10 CX37/Brockhouse, five CX37/Scottish Aviation and 25 CX37/Weymann. The CX19s were delivered in 1947/8, the CX37s in 1949/50 and 1953.

An irresistible Albion venture in 1960 consisted of an approximately 20-minute journey on service 1 between Argyle Street and Maryhill aboard a 1949 Roberts-bodied Venturer. The subdued sound from the Albion 9.9-litre engine and the pleasantly rhapsodic tones of the constant-mesh gearbox provided enjoyable accompaniment to travel, and I always thought that those Roberts bodies looked so well built and had a particularly pleasing rear end.

One Glasgow bus adventure that I just managed to avoid was stepping off a kerb in front of a rapidly-approaching LA1 — Glasgow's new and, at the time, only Alexander-bodied Leyland Atlantean. The original Alexander body for rear-engined chassis, although of somewhat boxy overall outline, at least lacked the rather bland-looking upper-saloon frontal countenance that characterised some other makes of bodywork for such chassis. Subsequent Glasgow Atlanteans — eventually to total more than 1,400 examples — were to have Alexander bodies incorporating curved glass at the front of both saloons and seemed so stylish and 'up-to-the-minute', obviously creating a favourable impression and doubtlessly enhancing Glasgow's image.

In 1960 Glasgow also had a Crossley — yes, just one of this most charismatic genus, a 1947 DD42 with constant-mesh gearbox and Manchester-style post-streamline Crossley body. Numbered C1, it never came out to see me, so it was as well that I'd seen and sampled numerous others of the type in England.

Travel 76 miles from Glasgow, and on the steep north bank of the silvery Tay you would find in the early and mid-1960s 245 municipal buses running around Dundee, population (then) 178,000 and my next neighbouring municipality. The tramway system had been abandoned during the 1950s, and the bus livery was of a shade that seemed to anticipate National Bus Company green, double-deckers having one relieving band of white at cantrail level.

Dundee's buses served such locations as Ninewells, Blackness, Sinderins, Downfield, Maryfield and Lochee. It was a pleasant surprise to note that among the provincial AEC Regent IIIs there were some former London Transport vehicles comprising 30 Cravens-bodied RTs along with 10 Weymann-bodied STL-class AEC Regent IIs altered from crash 'box to preselector. Upon hearing (from me) of these ex-Londoners my then boss, a hard-headed old Scot, was indignant: Huh! Did I think that any self-respecting Scottish city would have need of London's cast-offs?

Besides the AECs Dundee ran quite a mixed and attention-grabbing bag of Daimlers. The oldest, dating from 1943-5, were 16 CWA6s with Massey, Duple, Brush or Northern Counties utility bodies, their appearance somewhat altered by rebuilding that incorporated flush-fitting windows mounted in rubber. They were powered by the AEC 7.7-litre engine, a lively unit. Wartime utilities in general were relatively heavy, but with their gearing and quick, preselected upward ratio changes they were able to perform sportingly on Dundee's hilly terrain.

Daimler CW production continued for a time postwar, and in 1946 Dundee acquired three Duple utility-bodied CWD6s with the refined Daimler 8.6-litre CD6 engine. A further 20 similar chassis arrived in 1947, all with 56-seat Northern Coachbuilders bodies. These CWD6s were accompanied by three of the postwar CVD6 version in single-deck form plus two crash-gearbox AEC Regals, both types with 35-seat rear-entrance Weymann bodies.

Possibly the most eye-catching of Dundee's early-postwar deliveries were the 10 AEC Regent IIIs that arrived in 1948, bearing traditional sturdy Metropolitan-Cammell bodywork — smart performers with 9.6-litre engine and preselector 'box. Also delivered in 1948 were two further Weymann-bodied Daimler CVD6 single-deckers.

Barnard, of Norwich, was not a prolific builder of double-deck bodies, but in 1949 Dundee took 10 nicely-proportioned Barnard-bodied Daimler CVD6s, while in 1950 came nine similarly-bodied AEC Regent IIIs plus three Brockhouse-bodied chassis. Variety was extended even further in 1951 with the arrival of 10 Croft-bodied Daimler CVD6s and ten 30ft examples of the same chassis, fitted with 39-seat single-deck Brush bodywork.

A total famine in 1952 was relieved by a 1953 feast of four underfloor-engined 9.6-litre AEC Regal IVs with Weymann 44-seat front-entrance bodies, plus ten 56-seat Weymann-bodied Daimler CVD6s and seven AEC Regent IIIs bearing Alexander 58-seat bodies, the increased seating capacity being noteworthy. Only one new bus — a further Regal IV, with dual-door, 39-seat Alexander bodywork — arrived in 1954, but 1955 proved a bumper year, witnessing the delivery of 35 more Daimler CVG6s

Left: Wartime Daimlers survived in Dundee until 1965, albeit with their bodywork rebuilt, as apparent from the rubber-mounted windows on this 1944 Northern Counties-bodied CWA6, seen in service in 1964.
STEWART J. BROWN

with Metro-Cammell Orion bodywork of 60-, 64-or 65-seat capacity; these were Dundee's first double-deckers with Daimler's new-look frontal arrangements. However, 1956 saw the delivery of those 30 ex- London Transport 1949/50 Cravens-bodied AEC Regent IIIs. Apart from the effect created by the roof-mounted front route-number box they looked quite at home in Dundee and, indeed, were to last until 1968/69 — a bargain buy, what! Other 1956 deliveries, of a more routine nature, were six further Daimler CVG6s, with 65-seat Park Royal bodywork.

In terms of double-deckers the years 1957-64 represented an all-Daimler period for Dundee. Thirty more CVG6s, all with Orion-design Weymann-built bodies, were delivered in 1957, to be

followed in 1958 by a further 10 of the same chassis type with similar-looking Metro-Cammell bodywork; all were 65-seaters. Nothing else was delivered until 1960, which year saw the delivery of seven more CVG6s, these having not only the Manchester style of narrower bonnet and cowl but Alexander 65-seat bodywork with pleasantly rounded features, making an attractive-looking vehicle. In 1964 came 20 Fleetlines with 78-seat Alexander bodywork incorporating those modernistic features characterising Glasgow's contemporary Atlanteans. Another 20 joined the Dundee fleet in 1966, the same year witnessing the arrival also of 10 AEC Reliances with 53-seat Alexander bodywork and fitted with the optional semi-automatic gearbox featuring two-pedal control.

Some 60 miles further up the coast from Dundee, at the mouth of the rivers Don and Dee, lies Aberdeen. Some 40 years ago Aberdeen — population then 186,000 — and its not-so-near neighbour were similar in some aspects of their respective bus fleets, each having a relatively high age profile and also an emphasis on preselectors, meaning plenty of AECs and Daimlers. Aberdeen's livery was also green, albeit somewhat lighter than that of Dundee, with cream relief around the windows. Its fleet of around 250 buses, always well presented and maintained, shuttled between such locations as Bridge of Dee, Bridge of Don, Sea Beach, Northfield, Scatterburn, Torry and Kincorth.

Aberdeen had also replaced its trams with buses during the 1950s and in 1965 still had wartime Daimlers with rebuilt utility bodywork. I was fortunate that one of these, a 1944 Duple-bodied CWA6, turned up where I was waiting one day. Wonderful! There had been 14 such chassis, with Duple or Brush utility bodywork, plus 32 CWD6s, Aberdeen, like Dundee, having continued to take examples of the latter until 1947. Three delivered that year had single-deck bodywork by local coachbuilder Walker; they were joined in 1948 by four similarly-bodied CVD6s.

Also like Dundee, Aberdeen had AEC RT-type Regent III chassis, nine of them bought new in 1946/7, but with Weymann provincial-style bodywork, plus 10 similarly bodied 1949 Regent IIIs, a most appealing chassis/body combination. Interestingly Aberdeen also had four 1950 Crossley

SD42/7 synchromesh chassis with full-fronted 29-seat coach bodywork by Brockhouse.

Aberdeen's vast intake of 1950s buses included 111 Daimler CVG6s and 25 AEC Regent Vs. Five of the Regents were fitted from new with the optional Gardner 6LW engine in lieu of the standard AEC AV470 7.7-litre type; the others had AV470s, but due to high operating costs these were replaced after four years by Gardner 6LW units. Bodywork on the Daimlers was variously by Brockhouse, Weymann, Northern Coachbuilders, Crossley, Metro-Cammell Orion and Alexander, the AECs having Crossley, Park Royal, Met-Cam Orion or Alexander bodies. The period 1960-5 saw the delivery of a further 57 Daimler CVG6s, 12 bodied by Met-Cam, the remainder by Alexander.

The 1950s represented a period of increasing seating capacities, and from the fairly common double-deck total of 56 Aberdeen's standard rose during the decade to 66. This number of seats could be attained on a 27ft-long double-decker only by combining the maximum practicable upper-saloon total of 37 with 29 below, the latter figure being achieved by the fitting of a rearward-facing bench seat for five across the front bulkhead.

Almost half a century later, all has changed. What were once the Glasgow and Aberdeen municipal operations now form part of FirstGroup, while the successor to Dundee Corporation is National Express. Individuality is gone, and in its place have come the corporate identities of the 21st century.

Left: Aberdeen's fleet in the early 1960s was made up entirely of AECs and Daimlers. This RT-type AEC Regent III had a Weymann body.
STEWART J. BROWN

Right: The lines of the mid-1950s Crossley double-deck body had obvious Park Royal affinities, as illustrated clearly by one of Aberdeen's 20 Daimler CVG6s of 1954; 15 were bodied by Crossley and five by Metro-Cammell. ROY MARSHALL

Left: A wintry day in Aberdeen's Union Street in the late 1960s with a Metro-Cammell-bodied AEC Regent V heading west on cross-city service 1 between Auchinyell and Garthdee. Four decades later First Aberdeen service 1 still serves more or less the same route. STEWART J. BROWN

Below: The newest Daimlers in the Aberdeen fleet in the early 1960s were CVG6s with Alexander bodies. These were generally similar to buses being supplied to Glasgow but featured the later, wider version of the Manchester grille, had more seats (65, against Glasgow's 61) and opening front windows on the upper deck. DAVID WAYMAN

McGill's miscellany

Although it has been around only since 2001, Greenock-based McGill's — reviving the name of an old Paisley-area business — is now one of Scotland's biggest independent operators. **Billy Nicol** charts how the fleet has changed.

Left: McGill's was formed in 2001 to take over the Greenock operations of Arriva Scotland West, the successor to a number of major operators in the town — in turn Greenock Motor Services, Western SMT and Clydeside Scottish. Included in the vehicles taken over were a number of Mercedes-Benz minibuses. This one had UVG bodywork and is seen in Greenock bus station.

Below: To supplement the Mercedes a number of Optare MetroRiders was acquired from Arriva Yorkshire. This 31-seater had been new to West Riding in 1994.

Right: Bigger buses added to the fleet included this ex-Brighton & Hove Dennis Dart/Marshall.

Below: McGill's first new buses were six Dennis Darts with 37-seat Plaxton Pointer bodies, purchased in 2002. These were also the company's first low-floor vehicles.

Right: The Darts were followed in 2003 by six DAF SB120s with 39-seat Wright Cadet bodies. In 2007 they were joined by six similar three-year-old vehicles acquired from Eastbourne Buses.

Above: In 2005 McGill's expanded beyond local bus operation, introducing a range of summer-only long-distance leisure services. For these it purchased second-hand coaches, including this former Wallace Arnold Volvo B10M/Plaxton, photographed in Balloch. These services were branded 'Smoothiecruisers'.

Below: Full-size single-deckers were introduced to the fleet in 2006 with new Mercedes-Benz Citaros, one of which, also displaying 'Smoothiecruiser' branding, is seen in Glasgow on the service to Largs. By 2008 there were nine Citaros, constituting the biggest fleet of the type in Scotland.

Right: Alongside new purchases McGill's has in recent years also bought modern second-hand buses. These included three five-year-old Volvo B7RLEs with Wright Eclipse bodywork, acquired in 2008 from Minsterley Motors. This one, pictured outside Glasgow's Buchanan bus station, sports a revised fleetname style.

Left: In 2008 the company expanded by taking over some of the Paisley operations of First Stop. These now trade as United, as seen on this Marshall-bodied Dennis Dart, which started life in 1996 with Go-Ahead Northern. As a result of this the new McGill's company now operates buses from the Barrhead depot once used by the original McGill's business.

Left: And for those who remember the original McGill's business, this is a 1965 view at the company's depot in Barrhead. Nearest the camera is a Duple-bodied Guy Arab III, which survives in preservation, and alongside it a wartime Arab II with postwar Massey body and an ex-London Transport Cravens-bodied RT-class AEC Regent III.
STEWART J. BROWN

Back to front

The back end of a bus doesn't have to look like one — but **Peter Rowlands** reckons that on early rear-engined double-deckers it often did. He considers why and celebrates the diversity of this sometimes neglected feature of body design.

All photographs by the author

ERE'S THE THING of it. When rear-engined double-decker buses started to become commonplace in the early 1960s no one really knew quite what the back of a modern double-decker should look like. How should the rear windows and the engine compartment be arranged? How could proper engine access be reconciled with a smart appearance? How could you prevent the engine over-heating — or, at the very least, avoid roasting alive any passengers rash enough to sit in the downstairs rear seats?

You could argue that the designers basically got it wrong. What they came up with was the extraordinary protruding engine pod of the Leyland Atlantean and Daimler Fleetline, which made the engine compartment look almost like an afterthought. And that defined the appearance of a large proportion of British-built double-deckers for the next 20 years.

The problem was that the designers had no template to guide them. Previous double-decker buses had the engine at the front and stairs at the back. In the very early days the stairs tended to be tacked on outside the body proper — another kind of afterthought, almost literally. Eventually bodybuilders started to enclose the roofs, and the stairs were built into the body proper, but the basically ungainly look remained. The open platform inevitably gave the back end an asymmetric look, and the diagonal sweep of the stair rail added a

Left: A clue to the origin of the term 'back end of a bus': muddled and asymmetrical, yet oozing character if you only recognise it. In the 1970s and early 1980s this London ST, dating from 1930, ran on a sightseeing route across Central London. It is seen in Oxford Street in 1982.

Right: One of Manchester's impressive 'Mancunians' (left), in this case a Leyland Atlantean bodied by East Lancs, shows off its generously proportioned back windows and slimline side shrouds. The ex-Bolton Atlantean to its right was also bodied by East Lancs, but the styling was much more conventional for the time, though it had similar slimline shrouds. The pair are seen in 1981.

further jarring visual note. Little wonder, you might think, that the phrase 'like the back end of a bus' came to be used as a kind of music-hall term for 'ugly'.

When Leyland's designers were working on the rear-engined Atlantean they had not only to allow engine access and heat dissipation but also to address concerns about the 'bouncing' effect that would result from the heavy engine assembly hanging off the back of the chassis. Should they brace it by building it into the rest of the body structure or allow it to flex naturally, leaving the rest of the body alone?

They chose the latter course, and the rest, as they say, is history. In short, the back end of early rear-engined double-deckers still looked like ... well, like the back end of a bus. We came to live with the concept of the engine 'bustle' (the whole pod) and 'shrouds' (fairings between the pod and the overhanging upper deck), these latter introduced to give the body a more rectangular look — from the sides, anyway.

Opinions about these shrouds varied. Some operators insisted on them, others were quite happy to do without them. Some specified unusual variants — notably Manchester on its striking 'Mancunians'. The four builders that bodied these buses included shrouds to maintain the self-consciously square-cornered profile of the buses; but, unlike most, these shrouds were just metal plates of no significant width. At least one neighbouring operator — Bolton — specified similar slimline shrouds on quite different bodies; that Ralph Bennett was General Manager at Bolton and then at Manchester explains the similarity.

The shrouds were the obvious bits of the enthusiast's stock-in-trade, but there were other subtleties. Most notable, perhaps, was the broad, shallow triangular shape pressed into the top rear edge of the Leyland Atlantean's engine cover. On some vehicles 'LEYLAND' was applied to it in three-dimensional lettering, but even if this was absent (or was later removed) the shape was unmistakable and proclaimed 'Leyland' to all those in the know. Daimler Fleetline covers had no equivalent pressing. On later Atlanteans the triangular shape was replaced by a uniform horizontal strip, but the message was still there for those who needed it.

Although you might imagine that all Atlanteans and Fleetlines had conspicuous external engine pods, this wasn't actually the case, for a few operators experimented with full 'flat-look' back ends. In the early 1970s, for instance, Lancashire United Transport took a batch of Northern Counties-bodied Daimler Fleetlines on which the lower rear window was flush with the back of the engine compartment, while Northern Counties also rebodied some Fleetlines for Nottingham with flush rear ends. Here at last, it seemed, was the shape of back ends to come; but this didn't actually happen (in the Leyland camp, at least) until 1980, when the Olympian was launched to replace the Atlantean and Fleetline — and not completely until the new generation of low-floor double-deckers arrived, years later. However, Bristol Commercial Vehicles, latterly also part of the Leyland empire, bucked this trend. When, in the late 1960s, working closely with long-time bodybuilding partner Eastern Coach Works, it launched its rear-engined VR double-decker the body was given a

Left: A classic view of a DMS-class Leyland Fleetline in the London Transport fleet, with plain engine cover and shrouds to present a smooth side profile. This MCW-bodied bus is seen at Chipstead Valley in 1986.

Right: Rear view of the same bus, new in 1977, showing how the shrouds concealed an inset rear window and left space for the engine cover to be raised.

Below: For many years the Atlantean's engine cover featured a top pressing that served as a plaque for the Leyland name. Fleetlines never had an equivalent moulding. Photographed in Manchester's Piccadilly Gardens in 1980, a Northern Counties-bodied Atlantean (right) contrasts with an older MCW-bodied Fleetline.

flush rear end right from the start. Here was proof that the pod-effect design was not essential after all, mechanically or æsthetically. Intriguingly, because Bristol and ECW never espoused the pod effect in their own joint design, there was no appropriate engine cover to be used on VR chassis bodied by other manufacturers — hence, for example, the peculiarly mismatched ECW-style rear panel and upper-deck overhang on the VRs bodied by Metro-Cammell for West Midlands PTE in the mid-1970s.

Nottingham City Transport, by the way, played games more enthusiastically than any other operator

Above: **Yes — some Fleetlines *did* have flush, flat rear ends. This Northern Counties-bodied example from the Lancashire United Transport fleet is seen in Salford on a bright but wintry March day in 1982. Northern Counties was, incidentally, the first builder to use side shrouds to improve the appearance of rear-engined buses.**

Right: **The front view reveals that the LUT Fleetlines were not the most attractive products to have been built by Northern Counties.**

with the way Atlantean and Fleetline rear ends should look. In particular it persuaded bodybuilders (notably Northern Counties and East Lancs) to make the lower-deck windows much deeper than was the norm, and these were usually raked forwards from the top down. This undoubtedly made the interior much brighter, though one wonders at what cost in terms of the non-standard design.

You might think that when, as happened occasionally, builders were asked to provide single-deck bodies on rear-engined double-deck chassis, they would have found a happier way to integrate the engine compartment into the overall design; but alas no. At various times they came up with a succession of peculiar designs that continued to draw attention to the separate engine compartment.

Perhaps the most bizarre variation on the pod

effect came with the final batches of Fleetlines delivered for London operation. These featured a 'quiet pack' which included noise-reducing baffles built into 'stacks' in the position normally occupied by the side shrouds. The sloping grilles atop these stacks soon blackened with use, and ironically, many people felt that the mournful wailing emitted by the so-called 'quietening' system was actually more intrusive than the low-frequency sound waves it was meant to suppress. This was truly a case of misguided engineering triumphing over both form and function.

It was MCW that finally showed the world how the back of a stylish double-decker should look when in 1973 it launched its Scania-based Metropolitan integral, for on this — and on the Metrobus which followed — the rear end was conceived as a whole, the engine cover flush with the rear window.